From:

_____

Date:

_____

_____

The BIBLE
Promise
Book®
for the
Anxious
Heart

Written and Compiled by
Janice Thompson

BARBOUR BOOKS
An Imprint of Barbour Publishing, Inc.

ISBN 978-1-68322-945-2

Published by Barbour Books, an imprint of Barbour Publishing Inc., 1810 Barbour Drive, Uhrichsville, Ohio 44683, www.barbourbooks.com

Our mission is to inspire the world with the life-changing message of the Bible.

Contents

Introduction

What crazy, chaotic lives we lead—always on the go, many times weighed down by the cares of life. Anxieties can overwhelm us, stopping us short of our fullest potential in Christ. But God has a cure for anxiety, and it's found in His Word.

Check out this verse from Psalm 139:23 (NIV): "Search me, God, and know my heart; test me and know my anxious thoughts." God longs to take every burden, every care, and every anxious thought from us, giving us healing, comfort, and peace in their place.

This collection of Bible verses, prayers, and hymn lyrics should bring peace in difficult circumstances and encourage you when anxiety threatens to spoil your day. Each section opens with a prayer written specifically for a particular topic and closes with praise from a relevant hymn from days gone by.

This Bible Promise Book is in no way intended to replace regular Bible study or the use of a concordance for in-depth study of a subject. But if, for example, you are feeling frustrated, some of the Bible's wisdom and comfort is available to you here under the topic of Frustration. If you're in need of Contentment, there's a section for that too. For ease of use, topics are arranged alphabetically.

It's time to get beyond the feelings of anxiety and

find peace—true peace—in our Lord and Savior. What are you waiting for? Let's dive in and see what He has for us.

Abilities

I can do very little on my own, Lord. Oh, I try. I give it my best shot. But without You, my works come across as anemic and restricted. My abilities are limited when I lean on my own power. Breathe on me, Spirit of God, and infuse me with God-ability, so that I can impact this world I live in. Give me whatever gifts I need to touch those around me, Father. I want to reach them for You. Praise You, Lord, for entrusting me with abilities from on high. Amen.

Whatever you do, work heartily,
as for the Lord and not for men.
COLOSSIANS 3:23 ESV

We do not want you to be uninformed, brothers
and sisters, about the troubles we experienced
in the province of Asia. We were under great
pressure, far beyond our ability to endure,
so that we despaired of life itself.
2 CORINTHIANS 1:8 NIV

"Arise, for it is your task, and we
are with you; be strong and do it."
EZRA 10:4 ESV

Now to him who is able to do immeasurably
more than all we ask or imagine, according
to his power that is at work within us.
EPHESIANS 3:20 NIV

For this reason I also suffer these things, but I am
not ashamed; for I know whom I have believed
and I am convinced that He is able to guard
what I have entrusted to Him until that day.
2 TIMOTHY 1:12 NASB

Then Moses summoned Bezalel and Oholiab
and every skilled person to whom the LORD
had given ability and who was willing to
come and do the work.
EXODUS 36:2 NIV

And God is able to make all grace abound to you,
so that always having all sufficiency in everything,
you may have an abundance for every good deed.
2 CORINTHIANS 9:8 NASB

"Are ye able," said the Master,
"To be crucified with Me?"
"Yea," the sturdy dreamers answered,
"To the death we follow Thee."

Lord, we are able. Our spirits are Thine.
Remold them, make us, like Thee, divine.
Thy guiding radiance above us shall be
A beacon to God, to love and loyalty.

"Are Ye Able," Earl B. Marlatt

Acceptance

I'm accepted, Lord! You've welcomed me into the family, an adopted child now one of Your own. I don't have to be anxious about whether or not You care, Lord. You've made it abundantly clear: I'm not to be cast aside or overlooked. I'm a child of the King, ushered into the throne room to spend time with the One I adore. How grateful I am, Lord! Amen.

"Very truly I tell you, whoever accepts
anyone I send accepts me; and whoever
accepts me accepts the one who sent me."
JOHN 13:20 NIV

"These I will bring to my holy mountain and
give them joy in my house of prayer. Their
burnt offerings and sacrifices will be accepted
on my altar; for my house will be called a
house of prayer for all nations."
ISAIAH 56:7 NIV

The LORD has heard my supplication,
the LORD receives my prayer.
PSALM 6:9 NASB

"I gave them the words you gave me
and they accepted them. They knew
with certainty that I came from you,
and they believed that you sent me."

JOHN 17:8 NIV

Accept one another, then, just as Christ accepted
you, in order to bring praise to God.

ROMANS 15:7 NIV

"The Lord disciplines those he loves, and he
punishes everyone he accepts as his child."

HEBREWS 12:6 NCV

Loved with everlasting love,
Led by grace that love to know;
Gracious Spirit from above,
Thou hast taught me it is so!
O this full and perfect peace!
O this transport all divine!
In a love which cannot cease,
I am His, and He is mine.
In a love which cannot cease,
I am His, and He is mine.

His forever, only His;
Who the Lord and me shall part?
Ah, with what a rest of bliss
Christ can fill the loving heart!
Heav'n and earth may fade and flee,
Firstborn light in gloom decline,
But while God and I shall be,
I am His, and He is mine.
But while God and I shall be,
I am His, and He is mine.
"I AM HIS, AND HE IS MINE," GEORGE W. ROBINSON

Anxiety

I'm trying to lay it down, Lord. This anxiety has me wound up in knots at times, but today I make a conscious decision to rest in You. Show me how to do that so that my heart— so often riddled with anxious thoughts—can be at rest. Thank You, Father. Amen.

When anxiety was great within me,
your consolation brought me joy.
PSALM 94:19 NIV

Do not be anxious about anything, but in
everything by prayer and supplication with
thanksgiving let your requests be made known
to God. And the peace of God, which surpasses
all understanding, will guard your hearts
and your minds in Christ Jesus.
PHILIPPIANS 4:6–7 ESV

Anxiety in a man's heart weighs it down,
but a good word makes it glad.
PROVERBS 12:25 NASB

But the Lord answered her, "Martha, Martha, you are anxious and troubled about many things, but one thing is necessary. Mary has chosen the good portion, which will not be taken away from her."

LUKE 10:41–42 ESV

Humble yourselves, therefore, under the mighty hand of God so that at the proper time he may exalt you, casting all your anxieties on him, because he cares for you.

1 PETER 5:6–7 ESV

I have set the LORD continually before me; because He is at my right hand, I will not be shaken.

PSALM 16:8 NASB

It is useless for you to work so hard from early morning until late at night, anxiously working for food to eat; for God gives rest to his loved ones.

PSALM 127:2 NLT

Search me, O God, and know my heart;
try me and know my anxious thoughts;
and see if there be any hurtful way in me,
and lead me in the everlasting way.
PSALM 139:23–24 NASB

"And why do you worry about clothes?
See how the flowers of the field grow. They
do not labor or spin. Yet I tell you that not
even Solomon in all his splendor was dressed
like one of these. If that is how God clothes
the grass of the field, which is here today and
tomorrow is thrown into the fire, will he not
much more clothe you—you of little faith?"
MATTHEW 6:28–30 NIV

Wait and trust the LORD. Don't be
upset when others get rich or when
someone else's plans succeed.
PSALM 37:7 NCV

Peace to soothe our bitter woes
God in Christ on us bestows;
Jesus bought our peace with God
With His holy, precious blood;
Peace in Him for sinners found
Is the Gospel's joyful sound.

Peace to us the Church doth tell,
'Tis her welcome and farewell;
Peace was our baptismal dower,
Peace shall bless our dying hour;
Peace be with you, full and free,
Now and through eternity.

"Peace to Soothe Our Bitter Woes,"
Nikolai F. S. Grundtvig

Attitude

Whether I'm having a good day or a bad one, Lord, I can guard my attitude. It's not always easy, but I long to be the sort of person who greets each day with hope and joy leading the way. Help me, Father, with little nudges from on high. May I never forget that my attitude determines my altitude. I want to soar with You, Lord, with all anxieties cast aside! Amen.

Do all things without grumbling or disputing,
that you may be blameless and innocent,
children of God without blemish in the midst
of a crooked and twisted generation, among
whom you shine as lights in the world.
PHILIPPIANS 2:14–15 ESV

Do nothing from selfish ambition or conceit,
but in humility count others more significant
than yourselves. Let each of you look not only
to his own interests, but also to the interests of
others. Have this mind among yourselves,
which is yours in Christ Jesus.
PHILIPPIANS 2:3–5 ESV

Let us therefore, as many as are perfect, have this attitude; and if in anything you have a different attitude, God will reveal that also to you.

PHILIPPIANS 3:15 NASB

Our God is a God who strengthens and encourages you. May he give you the same attitude toward one another that Christ Jesus had.

ROMANS 15:5 NIRV

Finally, brothers, whatever is true, whatever is honorable, whatever is just, whatever is pure, whatever is lovely, whatever is commendable, if there is any excellence, if there is anything worthy of praise, think about these things.

PHILIPPIANS 4:8 ESV

For the word of God is alive and active. Sharper than any double-edged sword, it penetrates even to dividing soul and spirit, joints and marrow; it judges the thoughts and attitudes of the heart.

HEBREWS 4:12 NIV

Therefore, since Christ suffered in his body, arm
yourselves also with the same attitude, because
whoever suffers in the body is done with sin.

1 PETER 4:1 NIV

Praise to God; Oh! let us raise
From our hearts a song of praise;
Of that goodness let us sing
Whence our lives and blessings spring.

Praise to Him who made the light,
Praise to Him who gave us sight!
Praise to Him who formed the ear!
He our humble praise will hear.

Praise the mercy that did send
Jesus for our guide and friend:
Praise Him, every heart and voice,
Him who makes the world rejoice.

"PRAISE TO GOD, OH LET US RAISE," ELIZA FOLLEN

Brokenness

Father, so many times I've struggled with a broken heart. I couldn't see past my current situation to hopeful days ahead. I allowed the pain, the anguish of another's words or deeds to take me to the depths of despair, to a place where I felt separated from You and from those around me. I'm so glad You care about my broken heart, Lord. Every tear that has ever slipped down my cheek was noticed by You. You were right there, during every moment of anxiety and pain, brushing my tears away and cradling me in Your arms. Thank You for tending to my heart like a garden, Father. I'm so grateful for Your tender, loving care. Amen.

When you pass through the waters, I will be
with you; and when you pass through the rivers,
they will not sweep over you. When you walk
through the fire, you will not be burned;
the flames will not set you ablaze.
ISAIAH 43:2 NIV

The LORD is close to the brokenhearted
and saves those who are crushed in spirit.
PSALM 34:18 NIV

My sacrifice, O God, is a broken spirit; a broken
and contrite heart you, God, will not despise.
PSALM 51:17 NIV

He heals the brokenhearted
and binds up their wounds.
PSALM 147:3 NIV

David also said to Solomon his son,
"Be strong and courageous, and do the work.
Do not be afraid or discouraged, for the LORD God,
my God, is with you. He will not fail you
or forsake you until all the work for the service
of the temple of the LORD is finished."
1 CHRONICLES 28:20 NIV

But now, this is what the LORD says—he who
created you, Jacob, he who formed you, Israel:
"Do not fear, for I have redeemed you; I have
summoned you by name; you are mine."
ISAIAH 43:1 NIV

Broken in spirit
And laden with care,
Sweet is thy refuge:
Find it in prayer.

Tell it to Jesus,
Tell it to Jesus,
Tell it to Jesus,
He will give release.

Bear thy affliction,
Whatever it be;
Jesus thy Savior
Bore it for thee.
"TELL IT TO JESUS," FANNY CROSBY

Busyness

Whew! This life can be exhausting, Lord. Seems like I go, go, go around the clock. By the time I drop into bed, I'm so tired it's hard to spend time communing with You. Father, when my heart is overwhelmed and I can't keep up with it all, please show me how to slow down my busyness. Teach me to delegate. Show me how to let go of the things I don't need to be doing. I will thrive when I'm free to spend more time with You, Father. I need the rest that comes from being in Your presence. Help me, Father. Amen.

Now as they went on their way, Jesus entered a village. And a woman named Martha welcomed him into her house. And she had a sister called Mary, who sat at the Lord's feet and listened to his teaching. But Martha was distracted with much serving. And she went up to him and said, "Lord, do you not care that my sister has left me to serve alone? Tell her then to help me." But the Lord answered her, "Martha, Martha, you are anxious and troubled about many things, but one thing is necessary. Mary has chosen the good portion, which will not be taken away from her."

Luke 10:38–42 ESV

By the seventh day God had finished the work
he had been doing; so on the seventh
day he rested from all his work.
GENESIS 2:2 NIV

"Come to me, all who labor and are heavy laden,
and I will give you rest. Take my yoke upon you,
and learn from me, for I am gentle and lowly
in heart, and you will find rest for your souls.
For my yoke is easy, and my burden is light."
MATTHEW 11:28–30 ESV

I said, "Oh, that I had the wings of a dove!
I would fly away and be at rest."
PSALM 55:6 NIV

The LORD is my shepherd, I lack nothing. He
makes me lie down in green pastures, he leads
me beside quiet waters, he refreshes my soul.
PSALM 23:1–3 NIV

There is a place of quiet rest,
Near to the heart of God.
A place where sin cannot molest,
Near to the heart of God.

O Jesus, blest Redeemer,
Sent from the heart of God,
Hold us, who wait before Thee,
Near to the heart of God.
"Near to the Heart of God," Cleland McAfee

Calling

You've called me, Lord. What a remarkable concept! Your voice rings out across the craziness of this life, offering me a purpose. I'm part of a great team of believers who want to impact the world for You. Thank You for including me. This holy calling on my life inspires and uplifts and gives me an amazing sense of purpose. Point me in the direction You'd like me to go, Lord. I'm Yours—every gift, ability, desire, and joy conformed to that which brings You pleasure. Amen.

Who saved us and called us to a holy
calling, not because of our works but because
of his own purpose and grace, which he gave
us in Christ Jesus before the ages began.
2 Timothy 1:9 esv

Brothers and sisters, think of what you
were when you were called. Not many of you
were wise by human standards; not many were
influential; not many were of noble birth.
1 Corinthians 1:26 niv

And we know that for those who love God
all things work together for good, for those who
are called according to his purpose. For those
whom he foreknew he also predestined to be
conformed to the image of his Son, in order that
he might be the firstborn among many brothers.
And those whom he predestined he also called,
and those whom he called he also justified, and
those whom he justified he also glorified.

ROMANS 8:28–30 ESV

There is one body and one Spirit—just as
you were called to the one hope that
belongs to your call—one Lord, one faith,
one baptism, one God and Father of all,
who is over all and through all and in all.

EPHESIANS 4:4–6 ESV

I thank Christ Jesus our Lord, who has
given me strength, that he considered me
trustworthy, appointing me to his service.

1 TIMOTHY 1:12 NIV

We've heard the call to rally,
And we hasten to obey;
When Jesus needs our service,
We will heed without delay;
Redeemed with His own precious blood
On rugged Calvary,
We yield our all to Him.

"Rally!" is our watchword, "Rally" is our song!
All our time and all our power to Christ belong!
Rally, then with gladness, rally with a cheer,
We shall win the battle, for our captain's near!
"THE CALL TO RALLY," O. L. MARKHAM

Comfort

There have been seasons of my life, Father, when I felt so disconnected from You that I couldn't receive the comfort You were offering. Oh, but You swept in and penetrated my heart with Your Spirit, reminding me that I wasn't alone. You cared. You still care. That brings such peace to my heart, Lord, to know that You love me enough to intervene, to go to the depths with me. I'm so grateful for this amazing comfort that cocoons me, even now, Father. Amen.

Praise God, the Father of our Lord Jesus
Christ! The Father is a merciful God,
who always gives us comfort.
2 CORINTHIANS 1:3 CEV

The God of all comfort, who comforts us
in all our troubles, so that we can comfort
those in any trouble with the comfort we
ourselves receive from God. For just as we
share abundantly in the sufferings of Christ,
so also our comfort abounds through Christ.
2 CORINTHIANS 1:3–5 NIV

So the church throughout all Judea and Galilee
and Samaria enjoyed peace, being built up;
and going on in the fear of the Lord and in the
comfort of the Holy Spirit, it continued to increase.

ACTS 9:31 NASB

Shout for joy, you heavens; rejoice, you
earth; burst into song, you mountains!
For the LORD comforts his people and will
have compassion on his afflicted ones.

ISAIAH 49:13 NIV

Now may our Lord Jesus Christ Himself and
God our Father, who has loved us and given
us eternal comfort and good hope by grace.

2 THESSALONIANS 2:16 NASB

The Spirit of the LORD God has taken
control of me! The LORD has chosen and
sent me to tell the oppressed the good news,
to heal the brokenhearted, and to announce
freedom for prisoners and captives.

ISAIAH 61:1 CEV

You will increase my honor and
comfort me once more.
PSALM 71:21 NIV

Comfort, comfort my people,
says your God.
ISAIAH 40:1 NIV

For just as the sufferings of Christ
are ours in abundance, so also our
comfort is abundant through Christ.
2 CORINTHIANS 1:5 NASB

Comfort, comfort ye My people,
Speak ye peace, thus saith our God;
Comfort those who sit in darkness,
Mourning 'neath their sorrow's load;
Speak ye to Jerusalem
Of the peace that waits for them;
Tell her that her sins I cover,
And her warfare now is over.
"COMFORT, COMFORT YE MY PEOPLE," JOHANNES G. OLEARIUS

Conflict

This world needs a lot less conflict, Lord. It's no fun being at odds with friends or loved ones. That's why I'm so dependent on You during those seasons. You ease my anxieties and remind me that You are the Great Resolver. In an instant, You can turn things around and bring peace to a tumultuous situation. How grateful I am for Your intervention during these rough seasons, Lord. Thank You so much! Amen.

A gentle answer turns away wrath,
but a harsh word stirs up anger.
PROVERBS 15:1 NIV

Why do you fight and argue with each other?
Isn't it because you are full of selfish desires that
fight to control your body? You want something
you don't have, and you will do anything to get it.
You will even kill! But you still cannot get what
you want, and you won't get it by fighting and
arguing. You should pray for it. Yet even when
you do pray, your prayers are not answered,
because you pray just for selfish reasons.
JAMES 4:1–3 CEV

"If your brother sins against you, go and tell him his fault, between you and him alone. If he listens to you, you have gained your brother. But if he does not listen, take one or two others along with you, that every charge may be established by the evidence of two or three witnesses. If he refuses to listen to them, tell it to the church. And if he refuses to listen even to the church, let him be to you as a Gentile and a tax collector."

MATTHEW 18:15–17 ESV

Let all bitterness and wrath and anger and clamor and slander be put away from you, along with all malice. Be kind to one another, tenderhearted, forgiving one another, as God in Christ forgave you.

EPHESIANS 4:31–32 ESV

Lo, the conflict of the ages
Is upon us today,
And the armies are assembling
All in battle array;
Are you numbered with the faithful,
One of God's loyal few,
Who have sworn Him full allegiance?
Can He count upon you?

Have your eyes caught the vision?
Have your hearts felt the thrill?
To the call of the Master
Do you answer, "I will"?
For the conflict of the ages,
Told by prophets and by sages,
In its fury is upon us,
Is upon us today.

"The Conflict of the Ages," Lelia N. Morris

Contentment

I want to be okay with it, Lord. Whatever You've got next for me. . .help me to accept it. I want to be content to see where You will take me because I've watched You move in my life in the past. You meet every need and satisfy my soul beyond anything I could imagine. So there should be no fear as I look ahead. No anxieties. No uneasy feelings. Just peace, contentment, and trust. I will choose to rest easy in You and to accept Your perfect will for my life. Amen.

Not that I speak from want, for I have learned
to be content in whatever circumstances I am.
PHILIPPIANS 4:11 NASB

I know how to get along with humble means,
and I also know how to live in prosperity;
in any and every circumstance I have learned
the secret of being filled and going hungry,
both of having abundance and suffering need.
PHILIPPIANS 4:12 NASB

Now godliness with contentment is great gain.
1 TIMOTHY 6:6 NKJV

He will give grass in your fields for your cattle,
and you will eat and be satisfied.
DEUTERONOMY 11:15 NASB

The afflicted will eat and be satisfied;
those who seek Him will praise the
LORD. Let your heart live forever!
PSALM 22:26 NASB

Keep your lives free from the love of
money and be content with what you
have, because God has said, "Never will
I leave you; never will I forsake you."
HEBREWS 13:5 NIV

But if we have food and clothing,
we will be content with that.
1 TIMOTHY 6:8 NIV

I have made myself calm and content like a young child in its mother's arms. Deep down inside me, I am as content as a young child.
PSALM 131:2 NIRV

My soul is resting in God's peace,
Without a doubt or fear;
The boisterous waves of trouble cease,
For Christ, my Lord, is near.

Resting, resting,
Resting in God's sweet peace;
Resting, resting,
I'm resting in God's sweet peace.

The Spirit poureth from on high,
A sanctifying tide,
And bathing in its streams of joy,
My soul is satisfied.
"RESTING IN GOD'S PEACE," THOMAS M. MAGEE

Courage

Sometimes my knees knock together, Lord. I'm anxious and afraid. But then I read Your Word and I see the many men and women who dared to look their enemies in the face. I'm reminded that courage has its benefits. Today, I ask You to stiffen my backbone and square my shoulders that I might have the courage for the tasks ahead. You can do what I cannot. I'm so grateful, Lord, for Your supernatural boldness. Amen.

"Have I not commanded you? Be strong
and courageous. Do not be frightened,
and do not be dismayed, for the LORD
your God is with you wherever you go."
JOSHUA 1:9 ESV

My friends, the blood of Jesus gives us courage
to enter the most holy place by a new way that
leads to life! And this way takes us through
the curtain that is Christ himself.
HEBREWS 10:19–20 CEV

The wicked flee when no one pursues,
but the righteous are bold as a lion.

PROVERBS 28:1 ESV

Now when they saw the boldness of Peter and
John, and perceived that they were uneducated,
common men, they were astonished. And they
recognized that they had been with Jesus.

ACTS 4:13 ESV

The following night the Lord stood near
Paul and said, "Take courage! As you
have testified about me in Jerusalem,
so you must also testify in Rome."

ACTS 23:11 NIV

"Be strong and courageous. Do not be afraid
or terrified because of them, for the LORD
your God goes with you; he will never
leave you nor forsake you."

DEUTERONOMY 31:6 NIV

So men, have courage. I trust in God that
everything will happen as his angel told me.
ACTS 27:25 NCV

Be on your guard. Remain
strong in the faith. Be brave.
1 CORINTHIANS 16:13 NIRV

O courage, my soul, and let us journey on,
For tho' the night is dark, it won't be very long.
O thanks be to God, the morning light appears,
And the storm is passing over, Hallelujah!

Hallelujah! Hallelujah!
The storm is passing over,
Hallelujah!

The stars have disappeared, and distant lights are dim,
My soul is filled with fears, the seas are breaking in.
I hear the Master cry, "Be not afraid, 'tis I,"
And the storm is passing over, Hallelujah!
"THE STORM IS PASSING OVER," CHARLES A. TINDLEY

Crime

This world is frightening at times, Lord. I turn on the news, then quiver and quake at the stories I see. I know that I can rest easy with You, but I also know that I need to be aware of my surroundings so that I can stay safe. Thank You for bringing peace to my heart, even when evil ones are at work around me. I'm grateful for Your peace in the middle of the storm, Father. Amen.

Beloved, never avenge yourselves, but leave
it to the wrath of God, for it is written,
"Vengeance is mine, I will repay, says the Lord."
ROMANS 12:19 ESV

There are six things the LORD hates, seven
that are detestable to him: haughty eyes,
a lying tongue, hands that shed innocent
blood, a heart that devises wicked schemes,
feet that are quick to rush into evil, a false
witness who pours out lies and a person
who stirs up conflict in the community.
PROVERBS 6:16–19 NIV

People who oppose the authorities are opposing
what God has done, and they will be punished.
Rulers are a threat to evil people, not to good
people. There is no need to be afraid of the
authorities. Just do right, and they will praise you
for it. After all, they are God's servants, and it is
their duty to help you. If you do something wrong,
you ought to be afraid, because these rulers have
the right to punish you. They are God's servants
who punish criminals to show how angry God is.
ROMANS 13:2–4 CEV

Although a wicked person who commits
a hundred crimes may live a long time,
I know that it will go better with those
who fear God, who are reverent before him.
ECCLESIASTES 8:12 NIV

"You have heard that it was said, 'An eye for an eye and a tooth for a tooth.' But I say to you, Do not resist the one who is evil. But if anyone slaps you on the right cheek, turn to him the other also."

MATTHEW 5:38–39 ESV

The evils that beset our path,
Who can prevent or cure?
We stand upon the brink of death
When most we seem secure.

Since sin has filled the earth with woe,
And creatures fade and die;
Lord, wean our hearts from things below,
And fix our hopes on high.

"THE EVILS THAT BESET OUR PATH," JOHN NEWTON

Faith

Today I come to You with microscopic faith, Lord. I don't have much, but it's enough to stir You to action on my behalf. This tiny bit of faith can move mountains in my life and see me through the deepest valleys. It propels me to do great things for Your Kingdom. It gives me reason to hope again, even when I'm feeling hopeless. This faith is all I need to hang on when times are tough, so I'm hanging tight today, Lord. Praise You! Amen.

Faith means being sure of the things we hope for and knowing that something is real even if we do not see it. Faith is the reason we remember great people who lived in the past. It is by faith we understand that the whole world was made by God's command so what we see was made by something that cannot be seen.
HEBREWS 11:1–3 NCV

Jesus turned and saw her. "Dear woman, don't give up hope," he said. "Your faith has healed you." The woman was healed at that moment.
MATTHEW 9:22 NIRV

"And whatever you ask in prayer,
you will receive, if you have faith."
MATTHEW 21:22 ESV

Then he touched their eyes and said,
"According to your faith let it be done to you."
MATTHEW 9:29 NIV

He said to them, "Because of your little faith.
For truly, I say to you, if you have faith like a
grain of mustard seed, you will say to this
mountain, 'Move from here to there,' and it will
move, and nothing will be impossible for you."
MATTHEW 17:20 ESV

"Have faith in God," Jesus answered.
MARK 11:22 NIV

First, I thank my God through Jesus Christ
for you all, because your faith is being
proclaimed throughout the whole world.
ROMANS 1:8 NASB

Be watchful, stand firm in the
faith, act like men, be strong.
1 CORINTHIANS 16:13 ESV

Encamped along the hills of light,
Ye Christian soldiers, rise.
And press the battle ere the night
Shall veil the glowing skies.
Against the foe in vales below
Let all our strength be hurled.
Faith is the victory, we know,
That overcomes the world.

Faith is the victory! Faith is the victory!
O glorious victory, that overcomes the world.
"FAITH IS THE VICTORY," JOHN H. YATES

Family

I'm so grateful for the people You've placed in my inner circle, God—the ones who are blood related and the ones who pour into my life as if they were. These family members are my support group, my encouragement, my joy. I don't know where I'd be without them. I'm also grateful for the family of faith—Your church. All around this globe, my brothers and sisters join together, a mighty army of faith, a force to be reckoned with. How amazing to be a part of this family. Amen.

But he rescues the poor from trouble and
increases their families like flocks of sheep.
PSALM 107:41 NLT

Children, obey your parents in the Lord,
for this is right. Honor your father and
mother (which is the first commandment
with a promise), so that it may be well with
you, and that you may live long on the earth.
EPHESIANS 6:1–3 NASB

Your wife shall be like a fruitful vine
within your house, your children
like olive plants around your table.
PSALM 128:3 NASB

Both the one who makes people holy
and those who are made holy are of the
same family. So Jesus is not ashamed
to call them brothers and sisters.
HEBREWS 2:11 NIV

Whoever troubles his own household
will inherit the wind, and the fool will
be servant to the wise of heart.
PROVERBS 11:29 ESV

"And everyone who has left houses or brothers
or sisters or father or mother or children or
farms for My name's sake, will receive many
times as much, and will inherit eternal life."
MATTHEW 19:29 NASB

Therefore, as we have opportunity, let us
do good to all people, especially to those
who belong to the family of believers.
GALATIANS 6:10 NIV

They replied, "Believe in the Lord Jesus, and
you will be saved—you and your household."
ACTS 16:31 NIV

God bless the home, tho' humble,
So full of love's sweet light;
God bless the little children,
With their sweet faces bright;
God bless the mother tender,
God bless the father, too;
God make us fond and faithful,
God keep us kind and true.
"GOD BLESS THE HOME," TASSO CORBEN

Fear

*We humans struggle with fear, Lord, but I refuse to give in
to it. I'm so grateful for the many times You've lifted my
head and given me courage to forge ahead, no matter how
fearful the road. You've strengthened me from the inside
out. So today I look fear in the face and speak to it with
all the courage I can muster: "Be gone, in Jesus' name!"
Amen.*

For God gave us a spirit not of fear
but of power and love and self-control.
2 TIMOTHY 1:7 ESV

I sought the LORD, and he answered me;
he delivered me from all my fears.
PSALM 34:4 NIV

Fear not, for I am with you; be not
dismayed, for I am your God; I will
strengthen you, I will help you, I will
uphold you with my righteous right hand.
ISAIAH 41:10 ESV

"I tell you, my friends, do not be afraid of those who kill the body and after that can do no more. But I will show you whom you should fear: Fear him who, after your body has been killed, has authority to throw you into hell. Yes, I tell you, fear him."

LUKE 12:4–5 NIV

You, LORD, are the light that keeps me safe. I am not afraid of anyone. You protect me, and I have no fears. Brutal people may attack and try to kill me, but they will stumble. Fierce enemies may attack, but they will fall. Armies may surround me, but I won't be afraid; war may break out, but I will trust you.

PSALM 27:1–3 CEV

He is not afraid of bad news; his heart is firm, trusting in the LORD. His heart is steady; he will not be afraid, until he looks in triumph on his adversaries.

PSALM 112:7–8 ESV

Fear of man will prove to be a snare,
but whoever trusts in the LORD is kept safe.
PROVERBS 29:25 NIV

Fear not! God is thy shield,
And He thy great reward;
His might has won the field—
Thy strength is in the Lord.

Fear not! 'tis God's own voice
That speaks to thee this word;
Lift up thy head, rejoice
In Jesus Christ thy Lord.

Fear not! for God has heard
The cry of thy distress;
The water of His Word
Thy fainting soul shall bless.
"FEAR NOT," EDWARD G. TAYLOR

Finances

Lord, my financial needs seem huge at times. The proverbial mountains feel insurmountable. But I choose to focus on You, not my lack. You are Jehovah Jireh, my Provider. You know what I need and You've made provision, even before I ask. Your ability to make that provision is unlimited, unlike my ability, which pales in comparison. What an awesome and generous God You are, caring for the needs of Your children across this globe. I'm so grateful. Amen.

And my God will supply every need of yours according to his riches in glory in Christ Jesus.
PHILIPPIANS 4:19 ESV

Command those who are rich in this present world not to be arrogant nor to put their hope in wealth, which is so uncertain, but to put their hope in God, who richly provides us with everything for our enjoyment.
1 TIMOTHY 6:17 NIV

This is the way he governs the nations and provides food in abundance.
JOB 36:31 NIV

Our barns will be filled with every kind
of provision. Our sheep will increase by
thousands, by tens of thousands in our fields.
Psalm 144:13 niv

"If you, then, though you are evil, know how
to give good gifts to your children, how much
more will your Father in heaven give good
gifts to those who ask him!"
Matthew 7:11 niv

I have been young, and now am old,
yet I have not seen the righteous forsaken
or his children begging for bread.
Psalm 37:25 esv

"Consider the ravens: they neither sow nor
reap, they have neither storehouse nor barn,
and yet God feeds them. Of how much
more value are you than the birds!"
Luke 12:24 esv

Keep your life free from love of money, and be content with what you have, for he has said, "I will never leave you nor forsake you."
HEBREWS 13:5 ESV

Riches of earth I may not see,
God may prevent;
Riches of grace are offered me,
I am content.
Wealth of the world must fade and fail,
Earthly delights grow tasteless, stale,
I have the wealth that must avail—
Riches of grace.

Riches of grace forever endure;
Riches of grace my safety assure;
Riches of grace are fadeless and pure;
Riches of grace, riches of grace.
"RICHES OF GRACE," EDMUND S. LORENZ

Friendship

Lord, how I value the friendships of those You've placed in my life. They provide a shoulder to cry on, laughter when things are going well, comfort when my heart is heavy, and encouragement, no matter what anxieties I'm facing. May I be the kind of friend to others that they have been to me. And thank You, Father, for the ultimate friendship. . .with You. I know You will stick with me, no matter what—and I'm grateful. Amen.

Two are better than one, because they have
a good reward for their toil. For if they fall,
one will lift up his fellow. But woe to him who
is alone when he falls and has not another to
lift him up! Again, if two lie together, they keep
warm, but how can one keep warm alone? And
though a man might prevail against one who is
alone, two will withstand him—a threefold
cord is not quickly broken.

ECCLESIASTES 4:9–12 ESV

Iron sharpens iron, and one man sharpens another.

PROVERBS 27:17 ESV

"I will ask the Father. And he will give you another
friend to help you and to be with you forever."
JOHN 14:16 NIRV

A man of many companions may
come to ruin, but there is a friend
who sticks closer than a brother.
PROVERBS 18:24 ESV

The sweet smell of incense can make you
feel good, but true friendship is better still.
PROVERBS 27:9 CEV

A dishonest man spreads strife,
and a whisperer separates close friends.
PROVERBS 16:28 ESV

Whenever two or three of you come together
in my name, I am there with you.
MATTHEW 18:20 CEV

And let us consider how we may spur one
another on toward love and good deeds, not
giving up meeting together, as some are in the
habit of doing, but encouraging one another—
and all the more as you see the Day approaching.
HEBREWS 10:24–25 NIV

Faithful are the wounds of a friend,
but deceitful are the kisses of an enemy.
PROVERBS 27:6 NASB

A friend is always loyal, and a brother
is born to help in time of need.
PROVERBS 17:17 NLT

I need just such a friend as Jesus
To lead me on the upward way; A friend that
will be near When the darkest clouds appear,
Oh, I need just such a friend as Jesus.

I need just such a friend, One on whom I can
depend, I need just such a friend as Jesus,
A friend that will be true as no other one will do,
Oh, I need just such a friend as Jesus.
"THE FRIEND I NEED," EDWIN V. ADAMS

Frustration

How easily I'm frustrated, Lord! I know it's because I take on too much without asking for Your advice first. Today, I'm asking You to help me with these feelings of frustration, Father. Ease them, I pray. Calm my heart and give me peace. Amen.

Then, because you belong to Christ Jesus,
God will bless you with peace that no one
can completely understand. And this peace
will control the way you think and feel.
PHILIPPIANS 4:7 CEV

For God alone, O my soul, wait in silence,
for my hope is from him. He only is my rock
and my salvation, my fortress; I shall not be
shaken. On God rests my salvation and my glory;
my mighty rock, my refuge is God. Trust in him
at all times, O people; pour out your heart
before him; God is a refuge for us.
PSALM 62:5–8 ESV

"I have said these things to you, that in me you may have peace. In the world you will have tribulation. But take heart; I have overcome the world."

JOHN 16:33 ESV

Good sense makes one slow to anger, and it is his glory to overlook an offense.

PROVERBS 19:11 ESV

Refrain from anger and turn from wrath; do not fret—it leads only to evil.

PSALM 37:8 NIV

A hot-tempered man stirs up strife, but he who is slow to anger quiets contention.

PROVERBS 15:18 ESV

Cast your burden on the LORD, and he will sustain you; he will never permit the righteous to be moved.

PSALM 55:22 ESV

Do not fret because of evildoers
or be envious of the wicked.
PROVERBS 24:19 NIV

And let us not grow weary of doing good, for in
due season we will reap, if we do not give up.
GALATIANS 6:9 ESV

Troubled art thou? oh, be of good cheer;
Go and tell Jesus, He ever is near;
No anguish so deep, no trouble so dark,
But Jesus can bid it forever depart.

Go and tell Jesus, He ever is near;
Go and tell Jesus, have nothing to fear;
No anguish so deep, no trouble so dark,
But Jesus can bid it forever depart.
"GO AND TELL JESUS," ABNER BOWLING

Future

I don't know what's coming around the bend, Lord, but You do. And because I know You care about my every need, I'm convinced that my future is ripe with possibilities. Today, I choose to let go of any fears regarding the unknown. I place my hand in Yours and walk with confidence into all of my tomorrows. Lead me. Guide me. Energize me for the path ahead, I pray. Amen.

"Therefore do not worry about tomorrow,
for tomorrow will worry about itself.
Each day has enough trouble of its own."
MATTHEW 6:34 NIV

Come now, you who say, "Today or tomorrow
we will go into such and such a town and
spend a year there and trade and make a profit"—
yet you do not know what tomorrow will
bring. What is your life? For you are a mist that
appears for a little time and then vanishes.
Instead you ought to say, "If the Lord wills,
we will live and do this or that."
JAMES 4:13–15 ESV

Consider the blameless, observe the upright;
a future awaits those who seek peace.

PSALM 37:37 NIV

"Who is like me? Let him come forward and
speak boldly. Let him tell me everything that has
happened since I created my people long ago. And
let him tell me what has not happened yet. Let him
announce ahead of time what is going to take place.
Do not tremble with fear. Do not be afraid. Didn't
I announce everything that has happened? Didn't I
tell you about it long ago? You are my witnesses. Is
there any other God but me? No! There is no other
Rock. I do not know even one."

ISAIAH 44:7–8 NIRV

But those who hope in the LORD will renew
their strength. They will soar on wings like
eagles; they will run and not grow weary,
they will walk and not be faint.

ISAIAH 40:31 NIV

Your word is a lamp to my feet
and a light to my path.
Psalm 119:105 esv

For I am convinced that neither death nor
life, neither angels nor demons, neither the
present nor the future, nor any powers, neither
height nor depth, nor anything else in all
creation, will be able to separate us from the
love of God that is in Christ Jesus our Lord.
Romans 8:38–39 niv

Oh, I often sit and ponder,
When the sun is sinking low,
Where shall yonder future find me:
Does but God in Heaven know?
Shall I be among the living?
Shall I mingle with the free?
Wheresoe'er my path be leading,
Savior, keep my heart with Thee.

Oh, the future lies before me,
And I know not where I'll be;
But where'er my path be leading,
Savior, keep my heart with Thee.
"The Future," Jennie Stout

God, Our Father

Lord, what an amazing Father You are! You sweep people of every nation and tongue into the fold, loving each one— young, old, tall, short, bubbly, or shy. You are the best example we'll ever have of what a loving father should be like. You long for Your kids to spend time with You, and welcome even the ones who come wracked with guilt and shame. You cradle the broken in Your arms and whisper words of comfort and peace. You're a remarkable Father to all and Your children can rest easy, free from the cares of life, when they're curled up next to You. How grateful we are! Amen.

Because you are his sons, God sent
the Spirit of his Son into our hearts,
the Spirit who calls out, "*Abba*, Father."
GALATIANS 4:6 NIV

Do we not all have one Father? Did not one God
create us? Why do we profane the covenant of our
ancestors by being unfaithful to one another?
MALACHI 2:10 NIV

Yet you, Lord, are our Father. We are the clay, you are the potter; we are all the work of your hand.

Isaiah 64:8 niv

You should pray like this: Our Father in heaven, help us to honor your name.

Matthew 6:9 cev

But you are our Father, though Abraham does not know us or Israel acknowledge us; you, Lord, are our Father, our Redeemer from of old is your name.

Isaiah 63:16 niv

Jesus replied, "Anyone who loves me will obey my teaching. My Father will love them, and we will come to them and make our home with them."

John 14:23 niv

Give praise to the God and Father of our Lord
Jesus Christ! He is the Father who gives
tender love. All comfort comes from him.

2 CORINTHIANS 1:3 NIRV

Praise be to the God and Father of our Lord
Jesus Christ! In his great mercy he has given
us new birth into a living hope through the
resurrection of Jesus Christ from the dead.

1 PETER 1:3 NIV

Father, I stretch my hands to Thee,
No other help I know;
If Thou withdraw Thyself from me,
Ah! whither shall I go?

What did Thine only Son endure,
Before I drew my breath?
What pain, what labor, to secure
My soul from endless death!

"FATHER, I STRETCH MY HANDS TO THEE," CHARLES WESLEY

God, Our Rock

What an amazing image, Father! You are my rock, my fortress. You're solid, unmoving, not tossed about by every whim or fancy. Strong in the storm, sturdy under pressure, You won't let me down. I'm so grateful You've provided a place of safety that I can run to. No shifting sands with You, Lord! Thanks for being the most solid fixture in my life, Father! Amen.

Even our enemies know that
only our God is a Mighty Rock.
DEUTERONOMY 32:31 CEV

"My God is my rock, in whom I take refuge,
my shield and the horn of my salvation. He is
my stronghold, my refuge and my savior—
from violent people you save me."
2 SAMUEL 22:3 NIV

Who is God except the LORD?
Who is the Rock except our God?
2 SAMUEL 22:32 NIRV

Praise be to the LORD my Rock, who trains
my hands for war, my fingers for battle.
PSALM 144:1 NIV

"The LORD lives! Blessed be my Rock!
Let God be exalted, the Rock of my salvation!"
2 SAMUEL 22:47 NKJV

And they will say about you, "The LORD
always does right! God is our mighty rock."
PSALM 92:15 CEV

Our LORD and our God, you are my
mighty rock, my fortress, my protector.
2 SAMUEL 22:2 CEV

Since you are my rock and my fortress,
for the sake of your name lead and guide me.
PSALM 31:3 NIV

From a place far away I call out to you. I call
out as my heart gets weaker. Lead me to the
safety of a rock that is high above me.

PSALM 61:2 NIRV

But the LORD has become my fortress,
and my God the rock in whom I take refuge.

PSALM 94:22 NIV

"They are like a man building a house, who dug
down deep and laid the foundation on rock. When
a flood came, the torrent struck that house but
could not shake it, because it was well built."

LUKE 6:48 NIV

My hope is built on nothing less
Than Jesus' blood and righteousness;
I dare not trust the sweetest frame,
But wholly lean on Jesus' name.

On Christ, the solid Rock, I stand;
All other ground is sinking sand;
All other ground is sinking sand.

"MY HOPE IS BUILT ON NOTHING LESS," EDWARD MOTE

God's Presence

Father, I choose to run into Your presence today. There, in that holy place, I find peace, comfort, and healing. You wrap Your arms around me and remind me that You're in charge, that nothing happens without Your awareness. Thank You for letting me draw near, Father. I long to spend time with You, to see my life, my heart, my thoughts totally transformed. Heal me in Your presence, I pray. Amen.

The Lord replied, "My Presence will
go with you, and I will give you rest."
Exodus 33:14 niv

When all the people of Israel saw the fire
coming down and the glorious presence
of the Lord filling the Temple, they fell face
down on the ground and worshiped and
praised the Lord, saying, "He is good!
His faithful love endures forever!"
2 Chronicles 7:3 nlt

Then I was constantly at his side.
I was filled with delight day after day,
rejoicing always in his presence.

PROVERBS 8:30 NIV

"Sing and rejoice, O daughter of Zion!
For behold, I am coming and I will
dwell in your midst," says the LORD.

ZECHARIAH 2:10 NKJV

The LORD is in his holy temple; the LORD
is on his heavenly throne. He observes
everyone on earth; his eyes examine them.

PSALM 11:4 NIV

For the Lord himself will come down from
heaven with a commanding shout, with the
voice of the archangel, and with the trumpet call
of God. First, the believers who have died will rise
from their graves. Then, together with them, we
who are still alive and remain on the earth will be
caught up in the clouds to meet the Lord in the air.
Then we will be with the Lord forever.

1 THESSALONIANS 4:16–17 NLT

"Lo, I am with you always,
even to the end of the age."
MATTHEW 28:20 NKJV

He is not far from every one of us,
His power and wisdom shine from peak and plain.
The vaulted heav'ns outstretch a starlit fane,
Where hearts, where praiseful
hearts may worship Him.

He is not far from every one of us,
He nearer is than breath or feet or hands;
He dearer is than friend or home or lands,
The spirit's fount of joy, our soul's deep spring.

Oh! praise His name since He is near today,
Let whispered praise declare love's holy fear;
Let daily service speak the heart's full cheer,
The Lord is ours, the Lord is ours,
He is not far away.
"HE IS NOT FAR AWAY," R. A. CHASE

God's Word

It boggles my mind, Lord, that You spoke Your Word to followers who wrote it all down, that I might find life in You. The Bible isn't just a book filled with sage bits of wisdom, it's Your personal love letter to me—one that soothes my soul when I'm troubled and invigorates me when I'm in need of encouragement. What an amazing thing, that the Creator of all would pen such a precious letter to His children. I'm so grateful for Your Word, Lord. Amen.

But as for you, continue in what you have learned and have become convinced of, because you know those from whom you learned it, and how from infancy you have known the Holy Scriptures, which are able to make you wise for salvation through faith in Christ Jesus.

2 TIMOTHY 3:14–15 NIV

For whatever was written in former days was written for our instruction, that through endurance and through the encouragement of the Scriptures we might have hope.

ROMANS 15:4 ESV

Your eternal word, O Lord,
stands firm in heaven.
Psalm 119:89 nlt

All Scripture is God-breathed and
is useful for teaching, rebuking,
correcting and training in righteousness.
2 Timothy 3:16 niv

Until I come, devote yourself to the public
reading of Scripture, to preaching and to teaching
. . . . Persevere in them, because if you do,
you will save both yourself and your hearers.
1 Timothy 4:13, 16 niv

If you really keep the royal law found
in Scripture, "Love your neighbor
as yourself," you are doing right.
James 2:8 niv

Then he opened their minds so they
could understand the Scriptures.
Luke 24:45 niv

So faith comes from hearing,
and hearing through the word of Christ.
ROMANS 10:17 ESV

For I handed on to you as of first importance
what I in turn had received: that Christ died
for our sins in accordance with the scriptures.
1 CORINTHIANS 15:3 NRSV

The Bible stands like a rock undaunted
'Mid the raging storms of time;
Its pages burn with the truth eternal,
And they glow with a light sublime.

The Bible stands though the hills may tumble,
It will firmly stand when the earth shall crumble;
I will plant my feet on its firm foundation,
For the Bible stands.

The Bible stands like a mountain towering
Far above the works of men;
Its truth by none ever was refuted,
And destroy it they never can.
"THE BIBLE STANDS," HALDOR LILLENAS

Golden Years

What a precious Father You are! You care for me, not just in my "growing up" years, but even as I age. You see every wrinkle, every white hair, every aching joint. You're right there, Lord, to comfort and bring peace when I'm in my "golden years." Best of all, I know You'll never leave me as I grow older. What a blessed promise, Father! Amen.

Gray hair is a crown of glory;
it is gained in a righteous life.
PROVERBS 16:31 ESV

Yes, remember your Creator now while you
are young, before the silver cord of life snaps
and the golden bowl is broken. Don't wait
until the water jar is smashed at the spring
and the pulley is broken at the well. For then
the dust will return to the earth, and the
spirit will return to God who gave it.
ECCLESIASTES 12:6–7 NLT

Even to your old age I will be the same,
and even to your graying years I will bear you!
I have done it, and I will carry you; and I will
bear you and I will deliver you.

ISAIAH 46:4 NASB

Wisdom is with the aged,
and understanding in length of days.

JOB 12:12 ESV

So we do not lose heart. Though our
outer self is wasting away, our inner
self is being renewed day by day.

2 CORINTHIANS 4:16 ESV

O God, from my youth you have taught me,
and I still proclaim your wondrous deeds. So
even to old age and gray hairs, O God, do not
forsake me, until I proclaim your might to another
generation, your power to all those to come.

PSALM 71:17–18 ESV

The glory of young men is their strength,
but the splendor of old men is their gray hair.
PROVERBS 20:29 ESV

I have been young, and now am old,
yet I have not seen the righteous forsaken
or his children begging for bread.
PSALM 37:25 ESV

Be not dismayed whate'er betide,
God will take care of you;
Beneath His wings of love abide,
God will take care of you.

Through days of toil when heart doth fail,
God will take care of you;
When dangers fierce your path assail,
God will take care of you.

God will take care of you,
Through every day, o'er all the way;
He will take care of you,
God will take care of you.
"GOD WILL TAKE CARE OF YOU," CIVILLA D. MARTIN

Grace

*Your grace is truly amazing, Lord. I don't deserve it. So
many times, I've fallen short. But You extend it anyway.
Your riches are freely poured out in my life, and not at my
expense, but rather at the expense of Your Son. He did
what I could not do, Father! He gave Himself as a ransom
for my soul and covered every sin. When I deserved death,
He gave me life. When I deserved punishment, He offered
leniency. How grateful I am for this amazing grace,
Father! Amen.*

Let us then with confidence draw near to the
throne of grace, that we may receive mercy
and find grace to help in time of need.
HEBREWS 4:16 ESV

But he said to me, "My grace is sufficient
for you, for my power is made perfect in
weakness." Therefore I will boast all the
more gladly of my weaknesses, so that the
power of Christ may rest upon me.
2 CORINTHIANS 12:9 ESV

But my life means nothing to me. My only goal
is to finish the race. I want to complete the work
the Lord Jesus has given me. He wants me to tell
others about the good news of God's grace.

ACTS 20:24 NIRV

For sin shall not be master over you,
for you are not under law but under grace.

ROMANS 6:14 NASB

For it is by grace you have been saved,
through faith—and this is not from
yourselves, it is the gift of God.

EPHESIANS 2:8 NIV

Let your speech always be with grace,
seasoned with salt, that you may know
how you ought to answer each one.

COLOSSIANS 4:6 NKJV

For you know the grace of our Lord Jesus Christ, that though He was rich, yet for your sakes He became poor, that you through His poverty might become rich.

2 CORINTHIANS 8:9 NKJV

Amazing grace! How sweet the sound
That saved a wretch like me!
I once was lost, but now am found;
Was blind but now I see.

'Twas grace that taught my heart to fear,
And grace my fears relieved;
How precious did that grace appear
The hour I first believed.

Through many dangers, toils, and snares,
I have already come;
'Tis grace hath brought me safe thus far,
And grace will lead me home.

The Lord has promised good to me,
His word my hope secures;
He will my Shield and Portion be,
As long as life endures.

"AMAZING GRACE," JOHN NEWTON

Gratitude

When I think of all You've done for me, Lord, my heart is overwhelmed with gratitude! You've lifted me out of the miry clay and set my feet on a rock. You've provided for my every need. You've sheltered me from storms, defeated my enemies, and loved me with an everlasting love. I will never be able to voice with human lips the thanks I have for all You've done and all You are—but today I will do my best to try, through my words and actions. Praise You, Lord! I'm so grateful! Amen.

"But I, with shouts of grateful praise, will sacrifice
to you. What I have vowed I will make good.
I will say, 'Salvation comes from the LORD.'"
JONAH 2:9 NIV

Let the word of Christ dwell in you richly;
teach and admonish one another in all wisdom;
and with gratitude in your hearts sing psalms,
hymns, and spiritual songs to God.
COLOSSIANS 3:16 NRSV

Give thanks in all circumstances; for this
is the will of God in Christ Jesus for you.
1 Thessalonians 5:18 esv

In every way and everywhere
we accept this with all gratitude.
Acts 24:3 esv

Sing to the Lord with grateful praise;
make music to our God on the harp.
Psalm 147:7 niv

Oh give thanks to the Lord, for he is good,
for his steadfast love endures forever!
Psalm 107:1 esv

They risked their lives for me. Not only I but all the
churches of the Gentiles are grateful to them.
Romans 16:4 niv

For everything created by God is good, and nothing
is to be rejected if it is received with gratitude.
1 Timothy 4:4 nasb

We welcome this in every way and
everywhere with utmost gratitude.
ACTS 24:3 NRSV

Therefore let us be grateful for receiving a
kingdom that cannot be shaken, and thus
let us offer to God acceptable worship,
with reverence and awe.
HEBREWS 12:28 ESV

Lift up your jubilant voices,
All ye glad nations and sing;
Jesus the Savior is risen,
Jesus your Savior and king.

Jesus liveth! He hath risen,
Sundered the tomb
And conquered the grave;
Mighty Savior, live forever,
Jesus is king and He doth save.

Lift up your jubilant voices,
Greet Him with praises of joy;
Give to Him glory and honor,
Grandest of anthems employ.
"LIFT UP YOUR VOICES," MINNIE A. GREINER-EDINGTON

Grounded

Lord, I want to be rooted and grounded in You, not easily swayed by every temptation or wind of change, especially when I'm riddled with anxiety. May my roots run so deep that even the fiercest storm can't topple me. I long to know Your Word so fully that I can quote the verses by memory. I want to be so comfortable in Your presence that I long for it daily. Thank You for helping me in my quest to ground myself in You, Lord. Amen.

For the time is coming when people will not endure sound teaching, but having itching ears they will accumulate for themselves teachers to suit their own passions.

2 Timothy 4:3 esv

"But when he, the Spirit of truth, comes, he will guide you into all the truth. He will not speak on his own; he will speak only what he hears, and he will tell you what is yet to come."

John 16:13 niv

For this reason I kneel before the Father, from
whom every family in heaven and on earth derives
its name. I pray that out of his glorious riches he
may strengthen you with power through his Spirit
in your inner being, so that Christ may dwell in
your hearts through faith. And I pray that you,
being rooted and established in love, may have
power, together with all the Lord's holy people,
to grasp how wide and long and high and deep
is the love of Christ, and to know this love that
surpasses knowledge—that you may be filled
to the measure of all the fullness of God.

EPHESIANS 3:14–19 NIV

And he gave the apostles, the prophets,
the evangelists, the shepherds and teachers,
to equip the saints for the work of ministry,
for building up the body of Christ, until we
all attain to the unity of the faith and of the
knowledge of the Son of God, to mature
manhood, to the measure of the stature of the
fullness of Christ, so that we may no longer be
children, tossed to and fro by the waves and
carried about by every wind of doctrine, by
human cunning, by craftiness in deceitful schemes.

EPHESIANS 4:11–14 ESV

Do your best to present yourself to God as one approved, a worker who has no need to be ashamed, rightly handling the word of truth.

2 Timothy 2:15 esv

Into the heart of Jesus
Deeper and deeper I go,
Seeking to know the reason
Why He should love me so,
Why He should stoop to lift me
Up from the miry clay,
Saving my soul, making me whole,
Though I had wandered away.

Into the will of Jesus,
Deeper and deeper I go,
Praying for grace to follow,
Seeking His way to know;
Bowing in full surrender
Low at His blessed feet,
Bidding Him take, break me and make,
Till I am molded, complete.
"Deeper and Deeper," Oswald J. Smith

Health

Father, I'm so grateful that You care about my health, both physical and emotional. I can bring every need, every concern, every ache, every pain to You. You created this body and know exactly how it should run. Today, I submit myself to Your healing, Your glory in this body You've given me. Show me how I can better care for what You've entrusted to me, Lord. And thank You for the many times (and ways) You've already brought healing. Amen.

Do not be wise in your own eyes; fear the
Lord and shun evil. This will bring health to
your body and nourishment to your bones.
PROVERBS 3:7–8 NIV

Jesus went throughout Galilee, teaching
in their synagogues, proclaiming the good
news of the kingdom, and healing every
disease and sickness among the people.
MATTHEW 4:23 NIV

Dear friend, I pray that you may enjoy
good health and that all may go well with you,
even as your soul is getting along well.
3 JOHN 2 NIV

The LORD sustains him on his sickbed;
in his illness you restore him to full health.
PSALM 41:3 ESV

But for you who revere my name, the sun of
righteousness will rise with healing in its rays.
And you will go out and frolic like well-fed calves.
MALACHI 4:2 NIV

Heal me, O LORD, and I shall be healed; save me,
and I shall be saved, for you are my praise.
JEREMIAH 17:14 ESV

The words of the reckless pierce like swords,
but the tongue of the wise brings healing.
PROVERBS 12:18 NIV

Gracious words are a honeycomb,
sweet to the soul and healing to the bones.
PROVERBS 16:24 NIV

Praise the LORD, my soul, and forget not all his
benefits—who forgives all your sins and heals all
your diseases, who redeems your life from the pit
and crowns you with love and compassion.
PSALM 103:2–4 NIV

Savior give, oh, give me rest
For this torn and troubled breast;
Sin has bound me with its chain,
Come Thou Lamb for sinners slain.

Savior, heal, oh, heal me now,
As before Thy throne I bow;
All my tears cannot redeem;
Plunge me in the crimson stream.

Come, oh, come, with me abide,
Let me feel Thy blood applied;
Humbly at Thy feet I bow,
In my weakness heal me now.
"HEAL ME NOW," GEORGE C. HUGG

Hope

*Father, the enemy has tried to rob me of my hope so
many times, but I refuse to let him! Today, I choose to
cling to hope in every area of my life—health, provision,
relationships, and more. You are the great Hope-Giver,
Lord, the One who lifts my head when others leave me
downcast. Because I can trust You in every situation,
I know that good days lie ahead. I choose to place my
hope in You today, Lord, and praise You in advance
for the miracles yet to come. Amen.*

May the God of hope fill you with all joy and peace
in believing, so that by the power of the Holy Spirit
you may abound in hope.
ROMANS 15:13 ESV

For in hope we have been saved, but hope that
is seen is not hope; for who hopes for what he
already sees? But if we hope for what we do not
see, with perseverance we wait eagerly for it.
ROMANS 8:24–25 NASB

Hope deferred makes the heart sick,
but a desire fulfilled is a tree of life.
PROVERBS 13:12 ESV

We have this as a sure and steadfast
anchor of the soul, a hope that enters
into the inner place behind the curtain.
HEBREWS 6:19 ESV

There is surely a future hope for you,
and your hope will not be cut off.
PROVERBS 23:18 NIV

So we do not lose heart. Though our outer self
is wasting away, our inner self is being renewed
day by day. For this light momentary affliction
is preparing for us an eternal weight of glory
beyond all comparison, as we look not to the
things that are seen but to the things that are
unseen. For the things that are seen are transient,
but the things that are unseen are eternal.
2 CORINTHIANS 4:16–18 ESV

"The LORD is my portion," says my soul,
"Therefore I have hope in Him."
LAMENTATIONS 3:24 NASB

Hope on, hope on, O troubled heart;
If doubts and fears o'ertake thee,
Remember this—The Lord hath said,
He never will forsake thee;
Then murmur not, still bear thy lot,
Nor yield to care or sorrow;
Be sure the clouds that frown today,
Will break in smiles tomorrow.

Hope on, hope on, though dark and deep
The shadows gather o'er thee;
Be not dismayed; thy Savior holds
The lamp of life before thee;
And if He will that thou today
Shouldst tread the vale of sorrow,
Be not afraid, but trust and wait;
The sun will shine tomorrow.
"HOPE ON," FANNY CROSBY

Injustice

Lord, I must confess I'm not a fan of injustice. I know You aren't either. Sometimes I want to get angry when people are taken advantage of or wounded by others—especially when that wounding is intentional. Show me how I can be a light, so that the world sees Your heart in those moments. May I always be one who treats others fairly. I find comfort in the knowledge that You are a just God and will have Your way. . .in Your time. Amen.

Therefore the LORD waits to be gracious to you, and therefore he exalts himself to show mercy to you. For the LORD is a God of justice; blessed are all those who wait for him.
ISAIAH 30:18 ESV

Do not deny justice to your poor people in their lawsuits. Have nothing to do with a false charge and do not put an innocent or honest person to death, for I will not acquit the guilty.
EXODUS 23:6–7 NIV

"Be fair in your judging. You must not show special favor to poor people or great people, but be fair when you judge your neighbor."

LEVITICUS 19:15 NCV

The Almighty is beyond our reach and exalted in power; in his justice and great righteousness, he does not oppress.

JOB 37:23 NIV

He has told you, O man, what is good; and what does the LORD require of you but to do justice, and to love kindness, and to walk humbly with your God?

MICAH 6:8 ESV

I get my knowledge from far away. I'll announce that the God who made me is fair.

JOB 36:3 NIRV

When justice is done, it is a joy to the righteous but terror to evildoers.

PROVERBS 21:15 ESV

Learn to do good; seek justice,
rebuke the oppressor; defend the
fatherless, plead for the widow.
Isaiah 1:17 NKJV

But let justice roll on like a river,
righteousness like a never-failing stream!
Amos 5:24 NIV

A mighty fortress is our God,
A bulwark never failing;
Our helper He, amid the flood
Of mortal ills prevailing:
For still our ancient foe
Doth seek to work us woe;
His craft and pow'r are great,
And, armed with cruel hate,
On earth is not His equal.

Did we in our own strength confide,
Our striving would be losing;
Were not the right Man on our side,
The Man of God's own choosing:
Dost ask who that may be?
Christ Jesus, it is He;
Lord Sabaoth, His name,
From age to age the same,
And He must win the battle.
"A Mighty Fortress," Martin Luther

Jesus, God's Son

Father, I can't fathom what it must have been like for You, giving Your only Son. The pain, the anguish, the feelings of separation. . .how it must have ripped Your heart out. How grateful I am, Lord, for the gift of a Savior. Where would I be without Him? You knew exactly what I needed and sent the perfect One to stand in my place, to take my sins upon Himself on the cross. I can never thank You enough, Father. Praise You for Your Son! Amen.

"This Jesus is the stone that was rejected by you,
the builders, which has become the cornerstone.
And there is salvation in no one else, for there
is no other name under heaven given among
men by which we must be saved."
ACTS 4:11–12 ESV

Jesus said to him, "I am the way, and the
truth, and the life. No one comes to
the Father except through me."
JOHN 14:6 ESV

And being found in human form, he humbled himself by becoming obedient to the point of death, even death on a cross. Therefore God has highly exalted him and bestowed on him the name that is above every name, so that at the name of Jesus every knee should bow, in heaven and on earth and under the earth, and every tongue confess that Jesus Christ is Lord, to the glory of God the Father.

PHILIPPIANS 2:8–11 ESV

And the Word became flesh and dwelt among us, and we have seen his glory, glory as of the only Son from the Father, full of grace and truth.

JOHN 1:14 ESV

Jesus, my Lord, my God, my All,
Hear me, blest Savior, when I call;
Hear me, and from Thy dwelling place
Pour down the riches of Thy grace;
Jesus, my Lord, I Thee adore;
O make me love Thee more and more.

Jesus, what didst Thou find in me
That Thou hast dealt so lovingly?
How great the joy that Thou hast brought,
So far exceeding hope or thought!
Jesus, my Lord, I Thee adore;
O make me love Thee more and more.

"JESUS, MY LORD, MY GOD, MY ALL," HENRY A. COLLINS

Joy

Lord, Your joy really is my strength! Even on my lowest day, You supernaturally fill me with joy that bubbles up and pushes away pain, heartache, anxiety, and anger. In those moments, I'm reinvigorated. I get a heavenly injection that sees me through the situation. Thank You for pouring out joy, Father. I love the power that comes with it and the hope it brings. Today, no matter what I'm going through. . .I choose joy! Amen.

May the God of hope fill you with all joy and
peace in believing, so that by the power of
the Holy Spirit you may abound in hope.
ROMANS 15:13 ESV

Now rise up, O Lord God. Go to Your resting
place, You and the special box of Your power.
O Lord God, let Your religious leaders be
dressed in saving power. Let those who belong
to You be filled with joy in what is good.
2 CHRONICLES 6:41 NLV

You will make known to me the path of life;
in Your presence is fullness of joy; in Your
right hand there are pleasures forever.
PSALM 16:11 NASB

Rejoice in the Lord always;
again I will say, rejoice.
PHILIPPIANS 4:4 ESV

A joyful heart is good medicine,
but a crushed spirit dries up the bones.
PROVERBS 17:22 ESV

When anxiety was great within me,
your consolation brought me joy.
PSALM 94:19 NIV

Sing to him a new song; play
skillfully, and shout for joy.
PSALM 33:3 NIV

Make my joy complete by being of the
same mind, maintaining the same love,
united in spirit, intent on one purpose.
PHILIPPIANS 2:2 NASB

This is the day that the LORD has made;
let us rejoice and be glad in it.
PSALM 118:24 ESV

"These things I have spoken to you, that my joy
may be in you, and that your joy may be full."
JOHN 15:11 ESV

But I have trusted in Your loving-kindness. My
heart will be full of joy because You will save me.
PSALM 13:5 NLV

"The kingdom of heaven is like a treasure
hidden in the field, which a man found and
hid again; and from joy over it he goes and
sells all that he has and buys that field."
MATTHEW 13:44 NASB

O clap your hands, all peoples;
shout to God with the voice of joy.
PSALM 47:1 NASB

Joyful, joyful, we adore Thee,
God of glory, Lord of love;
Hearts unfold like flowers before Thee,
Praising Thee, their sun above.
Melt the clouds of sin and sadness;
Drive the dark of doubt away;
Giver of immortal gladness,
Fill us with the light of day!

Mortals, join the mighty chorus,
Which the morning stars began;
Father-love is reigning o'er us,
Brother-love binds man to man.
Ever singing march we onward,
Victors in the midst of strife,
Joyful music leads us sunward
In the triumph song of life.
"JOYFUL, JOYFUL, WE ADORE THEE," HENRY J. VAN DYKE

Love

What a gift, this precious gift of love is! When I'm feeling alone, washed up, wrung out, deep in grief, You step in and cradle me in Your arms, whispering words of love in my ears and giving me strength and courage to go on. I've never felt this safe, this comfortable, this reassured. And how can I ever thank You for the love You expressed when You sent Your Son? Jesus is the greatest love-gift I've ever received—and I'm so thankful! Praise You for everlasting love, Lord! Amen.

Let all that you do be done in love.
1 CORINTHIANS 16:14 ESV

Yet the LORD set his affection on your ancestors and loved them, and he chose you, their descendants, above all the nations—as it is today.
DEUTERONOMY 10:15 NIV

Hatred stirs up strife,
but love covers all offenses.
PROVERBS 10:12 ESV

Give thanks to the Lord, for he is good;
his love endures forever.
1 Chronicles 16:34 niv

But I trust in your unfailing love.
I will rejoice because you have rescued me.
Psalm 13:5 nlt

Surely your goodness and love will follow
me all the days of my life, and I will
dwell in the house of the Lord forever.
Psalm 23:6 niv

Because Your lovingkindness is better
than life, my lips will praise You.
Psalm 63:3 nasb

And above all these put on love, which binds
everything together in perfect harmony.
Colossians 3:14 esv

But as for me, I shall sing of Your strength; yes,
I shall joyfully sing of Your lovingkindness in
the morning, for You have been my stronghold
and a refuge in the day of my distress.

PSALM 59:16 NASB

Let those who fear the LORD say:
"His love endures forever."

PSALM 118:4 NIV

Wonderful love that rescued me, sunk deep in sin,
Guilty and vile as I could be—no hope within;
When every ray of light had fled, O glorious day!
Raising my soul from out the dead, love found a way.

Love found a way, to redeem my soul,
Love found a way, that could make me whole.
Love sent my Lord to the cross of shame,
Love found a way, O praise His holy name!
"LOVE FOUND A WAY," AVIS M. CHRISTIANSEN

Morality

Father, I want to walk in such close communion with You that my heart beats like Yours. May the things that concern You, concern me. May the things that bring You joy, bring me joy. May my conscience never be seared by this world. May I always care about the things that matter to You, Father. Guide and direct, I pray. Keep me within the boundaries of Your love, Lord. Amen.

Be diligent to present yourself approved to God
as a workman who does not need to be ashamed,
accurately handling the word of truth.
2 TIMOTHY 2:15 NASB

I appeal to you therefore, brothers, by the
mercies of God, to present your bodies as a
living sacrifice, holy and acceptable to God,
which is your spiritual worship. Do not be
conformed to this world, but be transformed
by the renewal of your mind, that by testing
you may discern what is the will of God,
what is good and acceptable and perfect.
ROMANS 12:1–2 ESV

"For this is the covenant that I will make with the house of Israel after those days, declares the LORD: I will put my law within them, and I will write it on their hearts. And I will be their God, and they shall be my people."

JEREMIAH 31:33 ESV

Owe no one anything, except to love each other, for the one who loves another has fulfilled the law. For the commandments, "You shall not commit adultery, You shall not murder, You shall not steal, You shall not covet," and any other commandment, are summed up in this word: "You shall love your neighbor as yourself." Love does no wrong to a neighbor; therefore love is the fulfilling of the law.

ROMANS 13:8–10 ESV

"So whatever you wish that others would do to you, do also to them, for this is the Law and the Prophets."

MATTHEW 7:12 ESV

But Peter and the apostles answered,
"We must obey God rather than men."
ACTS 5:29 ESV

Show me the way, dear Savior!
The shadows are falling fast;
And thro' the clouds above me
No ray of light is cast;
The storm is wildly raging,
The thunders loudly roar;
The restless waves are dashing
Against the wreck-strewn shore.

Show me the way, dear Savior
That Thou wouldst have me go;
Show me the way, dear Savior,
For Thou alone dost know.
"SHOW ME THE WAY, DEAR SAVIOR," ALICE T. CRISS

New Beginnings

It feels so good to start over, Lord. Yesterday is behind me. Gone. Washed away. I've put it out of my mind. It has no control over me. Anxiety has vanished. Today, my thoughts, motivations, goals, and desires are brand-new, thanks to You! How can I ever thank You for giving me a chance to erase the past, to begin again? I'm so grateful, Father! Amen.

Therefore, if anyone is in Christ, he is a
new creation. The old has passed away;
behold, the new has come.
2 CORINTHIANS 5:17 ESV

"Do not call to mind the former things,
or ponder things of the past. Behold, I will
do something new, now it will spring forth;
will you not be aware of it? I will even make a
roadway in the wilderness, rivers in the desert."
ISAIAH 43:18–19 NASB

And he who was seated on the throne said,
"Behold, I am making all things new."
Also he said, "Write this down, for these
words are trustworthy and true."
REVELATION 21:5 ESV

"'He will wipe every tear from their eyes. There
will be no more death' or mourning or crying or
pain, for the old order of things has passed away."
REVELATION 21:4 NIV

Blessed be the God and Father of our Lord Jesus
Christ! According to his great mercy, he has caused
us to be born again to a living hope through the
resurrection of Jesus Christ from the dead.
1 PETER 1:3 ESV

And your ancient ruins shall be rebuilt; you shall
raise up the foundations of many generations;
you shall be called the repairer of the breach,
the restorer of streets to dwell in.
ISAIAH 58:12 ESV

Begin the day with God!
He is thy sun and day;
His is the radiance of thy dawn,
To Him address thy lay.

Sing a new song at morn!
Join the glad woods and hills;
Join the fresh winds and seas and plains,
Join the bright flowers and rills.

Sing thy first song to God
Not to thy fellow man;
Not to the creatures of His hand,
But to the glorious One.

"Begin with God," Horatius Bonar

Obedience

*Sometimes I have felt like obedience is a drudgery,
something I had to do to make others happy. Now I
realize that obedience is a gift—one that keeps me from
needless anxieties! Walking safely within the boundaries
You've set, I stand a much better chance at a happy
future. Thank You for showing me that You're not a
cruel taskmaster. You're a loving, confirming Father,
who wants me to thrive in every way. How I praise
You as I choose to obey Your Word, Lord. Amen.*

If you are willing and obedient,
you shall eat the good of the land.
Isaiah 1:19 esv

Walk in obedience to all that the Lord your
God has commanded you, so that you may
live and prosper and prolong your days
in the land that you will possess.
Deuteronomy 5:33 niv

"If you love me, you will
keep my commandments."
John 14:15 esv

You have declared this day that the LORD is your God and that you will walk in obedience to him, that you will keep his decrees, commands and laws—that you will listen to him.

DEUTERONOMY 26:17 NIV

Blessed are all who fear the LORD,
who walk in obedience to him.

PSALM 128:1 NIV

As obedient children, do not be conformed
to the passions of your former ignorance.

1 PETER 1:14 ESV

I will always obey your law, for ever and ever.

PSALM 119:44 NIRV

He replied, "Instead, blessed are those
who hear God's word and obey it."

LUKE 11:28 NIRV

Whoever keeps his commandments abides in God,
and God in him. And by this we know that he abides
in us, by the Spirit whom he has given us.

1 JOHN 3:24 ESV

"And we are witnesses of these things;
and so is the Holy Spirit, whom God
has given to those who obey Him."

ACTS 5:32 NASB

But if anyone obeys his word, love for God
is truly made complete in them. This is how
we know we are in him: Whoever claims
to live in him must live as Jesus did.

1 JOHN 2:5–6 NIV

When we walk with the Lord in the light of His Word,
What a glory He sheds on our way!
While we do His good will, He abides with us still,
And with all who will trust and obey.

Trust and obey, for there's no other way
To be happy in Jesus, but to trust and obey.
"TRUST AND OBEY," JOHN H. SAMMIS

Parenting

Father, You're the best example we have of excellent parenting skills. You show how to discipline in love, guide with encouragement, and forgive when the situation calls for it. May I learn from Your example, that my parenting skills (whether I'm dealing with a son, daughter, grandchild, niece, nephew, or mentee) might be all they can be. Amen.

Train up a child in the way he should go;
even when he is old he will not depart from it.
PROVERBS 22:6 ESV

Fathers, do not embitter your children,
or they will become discouraged.
COLOSSIANS 3:21 NIV

Whoever spares the rod hates his son, but he
who loves him is diligent to discipline him.
PROVERBS 13:24 ESV

It is for discipline that you have to endure.
God is treating you as sons. For what son is
there whom his father does not discipline? If
you are left without discipline, in which all have
participated, then you are illegitimate children
and not sons. Besides this, we have had earthly
fathers who disciplined us and we respected them.
Shall we not much more be subject to the Father of
spirits and live? For they disciplined us for a short
time as it seemed best to them, but he disciplines
us for our good, that we may share his holiness.
For the moment all discipline seems painful rather
than pleasant, but later it yields the peaceful fruit of
righteousness to those who have been trained by it.
HEBREWS 12:7–11 ESV

As a father has compassion on his children, so
the LORD has compassion on those who fear him.
PSALM 103:13 NIV

Behold, children are a gift of the
LORD, the fruit of the womb is a reward.
PSALM 127:3 NASB

You shall teach them to your children, talking
of them when you are sitting in your house,
and when you are walking by the way, and
when you lie down, and when you rise.
DEUTERONOMY 11:19 ESV

Children sing, gladly sing,
Hallelujahs to our king;
Lord of all, great and small,
At His feet with rapture fall;
Children sing, He is near,
Bending still His gracious ear;
Trust in Him, O rejoice!
Praise the Lord with heart and voice.

Then sing, gladly sing.
Sing, gladly sing.
Till the heav'nly arches ring,
Till you hear the saints above,
Praising God, for He is love.
"CHILDREN SING," FANNY CROSBY

Patience

Lord, I have to confess that sometimes I'm not very patient. I want what I want when I want it. And when You (seemingly) don't come through for me, I get discouraged, anxious, or overwhelmed. How ashamed I am when I see Your answer for my issue, for it's usually better than anything I would've dreamed for myself. Help me, Father. May my patience grow and grow! Amen.

Rather, as servants of God we commend
ourselves in every way: in great endurance;
in troubles, hardships and distresses; in
beatings, imprisonments and riots; in hard
work, sleepless nights and hunger; in purity,
understanding, patience and kindness;
in the Holy Spirit and in sincere love.
2 Corinthians 6:4–6 niv

God will strengthen you with his own
great power so that you will not give up
when troubles come, but you will be patient.
Colossians 1:11 ncv

Therefore, as God's chosen people, holy and dearly loved, clothe yourselves with compassion, kindness, humility, gentleness and patience.

COLOSSIANS 3:12 NIV

You, however, know all about my teaching, my way of life, my purpose, faith, patience, love, endurance, persecutions, sufferings—what kinds of things happened to me in Antioch, Iconium and Lystra, the persecutions I endured. Yet the Lord rescued me from all of them.

2 TIMOTHY 3:10–11 NIV

Be patient, then, brothers and sisters, until the Lord's coming. See how the farmer waits for the land to yield its valuable crop, patiently waiting for the autumn and spring rains.

JAMES 5:7 NIV

Be joyful because you have hope. Be patient when trouble comes, and pray at all times.

ROMANS 12:12 NCV

But for that very reason I was shown mercy
so that in me, the worst of sinners, Christ Jesus
might display his immense patience as an
example for those who would believe in
him and receive eternal life.

1 TIMOTHY 1:16 NIV

Love is patient, love is kind and is not jealous;
love does not brag and is not arrogant.

1 CORINTHIANS 13:4 NASB

Be completely humble and gentle; be patient,
bearing with one another in love.

EPHESIANS 4:2 NIV

The Lord is not slow in doing what he promised—
the way some people understand slowness. But
God is being patient with you. He does not want
anyone to be lost, but he wants all people to
change their hearts and lives.

2 PETER 3:9 NCV

Our friends are gathering, one by one,
To meet the blessed Lord;
How soon this earthly journey's done,
And then the rich reward.

Wait, patiently wait,
Wait, patiently wait;
Wait for His coming,
Be it early, be it late.
"Wait, Patiently Wait," John Kurzenknabe

Peace

Only You can bring peace to difficult situations, Father. I've seen You do it time and time again. In the very moment when I'm knotted up inside and fear the worst, You sweep in with a cocoon of supernatural, inexplicable peace. You change everything—the way I'm feeling, my prospects for the future, my feelings about the situation I'm walking through. What a comforter You are, and how I praise You! Amen.

Now may the Lord of peace himself
give you peace at all times in every
way. The Lord be with you all.
2 THESSALONIANS 3:16 ESV

"Peace I leave with you; my peace I give you.
I do not give to you as the world gives. Do not
let your hearts be troubled and do not be afraid."
JOHN 14:27 NIV

You keep him in perfect peace whose mind
is stayed on you, because he trusts in you.
ISAIAH 26:3 ESV

"I have told you all this so that you may have peace in me. Here on earth you will have many trials and sorrows. But take heart, because I have overcome the world."

John 16:33 nlt

Let him turn away from evil and do good; let him seek peace and pursue it.

1 Peter 3:11 esv

He said to her, "Dear woman, your faith has healed you. Go in peace. You are free from your suffering."

Mark 5:34 nirv

In peace I will both lie down and sleep; for you alone, O Lord, make me dwell in safety.

Psalm 4:8 esv

"The LORD turn his face toward
you and give you peace."
NUMBERS 6:26 NIV

In perfect peace my heart is stayed,
On Christ the Lord divine;
My burdens are on Jesus laid,
And perfect peace is mine.

In perfect peace, in perfect peace,
Tho' storms around me roll,
My hope is fixed on Christ the Lord,
I've peace within my soul.

In perfect peace the Lord will keep
The weary and oppressed;
In waking hours, in deepest sleep,
By trusting Him, we rest.
"PERFECT PEACE," ALFRED W. HARE

Persecution

Father, many of us make it a life goal to avoid persecution. Still, I know that all who claim You as Lord will face troubles in this life. Those who don't know You could rise against me. During those rough seasons, I choose to trust in You and to stand faithful to the cause. Like those amazing disciples who've gone before me, I stand firm in my faith, even when the storms rage. Help me, I pray. Amen.

Indeed, all who desire to live a godly
life in Christ Jesus will be persecuted.
2 Timothy 3:12 esv

"If the world hates you, you know that
it has hated Me before it hated you."
John 15:18 nasb

For it is better to suffer for doing good, if that
should be God's will, than for doing evil.
1 Peter 3:17 esv

We are afflicted in every way, but not crushed;
perplexed, but not driven to despair; persecuted,
but not forsaken; struck down, but not destroyed;
always carrying in the body the death of Jesus,
so that the life of Jesus may also be manifested
in our bodies. For we who live are always being
given over to death for Jesus' sake, so that the life
of Jesus also may be manifested in our mortal flesh.
So death is at work in us, but life in you.
2 Corinthians 4:8–12 esv

Dear friends, do not be surprised at the fiery
ordeal that has come on you to test you,
as though something strange were happening to
you. But rejoice inasmuch as you participate in the
sufferings of Christ, so that you may be overjoyed
when his glory is revealed. If you are insulted
because of the name of Christ, you are blessed,
for the Spirit of glory and of God rests on you.
1 Peter 4:12–14 niv

For the sake of Christ, then, I am content with
weaknesses, insults, hardships, persecutions, and
calamities. For when I am weak, then I am strong.
2 Corinthians 12:10 esv

After the midnight, morning will greet us;
After the sadness, joy will appear;
After the tempest, sunlight will meet us;
After the jeering, praise we shall hear.

After the shadows, there will be sunshine;
After the frown, the soul-cheering smile;
Cling to the Savior, love Him forever;
All will be well in a little while.
"AFTER THE MIDNIGHT," JAMES ROWE

Plans

*You have amazing plans for me, Lord, and I can't wait
to see where the road will take me. While I'm waiting, I
choose to trust. Anything I could dream up for myself pales
in comparison to what You have in store. So, I won't get
anxious. I won't try to fit square pegs into round holes. I'll
wait to see what amazing things are coming around the
bend, then rest easy in the notion that You've planned it
all, just for me. Amen!*

Commit your work to the LORD,
and your plans will be established.
PROVERBS 16:3 ESV

"For I know the plans I have for you," declares
the LORD, "plans to prosper you and not to harm
you, plans to give you hope and a future."
JEREMIAH 29:11 NIV

The heart of man plans his way,
but the LORD establishes his steps.
PROVERBS 16:9 ESV

The plans of the diligent lead surely
to abundance, but everyone who
is hasty comes only to poverty.
PROVERBS 21:5 ESV

Many are the plans in the mind of a man,
but it is the purpose of the LORD that will stand.
PROVERBS 19:21 ESV

Come now, you who say, "Today or tomorrow
we will go into such and such a town and
spend a year there and trade and make a
profit"—yet you do not know what tomorrow will
bring. What is your life? For you are a mist
that appears for a little time and then vanishes.
Instead you ought to say, "If the Lord wills,
we will live and do this or that."
JAMES 4:13–15 ESV

"But seek first the kingdom of God
and his righteousness, and all these
things will be added to you."
MATTHEW 6:33 ESV

Though the way seems straight and narrow,
All I claimed was swept away;
My ambitions, plans and wishes,
At my feet in ashes lay.

Then God's fire upon the altar
Of my heart was set aflame;
I shall never cease to praise Him,
Glory, glory to His name.

I will praise Him! I will praise Him!
Praise the Lamb for sinners slain;
Give Him glory, all ye people,
For His blood can wash away each stain.
"I WILL PRAISE HIM," MARGARET J. HARRIS

Praise

There is none worthier of praise than You, Lord! How often I forget to pause and thank You for blue skies, a car that runs, money to pay my bills, and my health. Even when the skies are gray, You are still worthy, for You are the Author and Creator of all. Today, I choose to dig deep and offer a sacrifice of praise, even for those areas of my life that seem to be in disarray. You are my God, my King, my Provider, the Love of my life. You, oh Lord, are worthy of my highest praise! Amen.

Sing joyfully to the LORD, you righteous;
it is fitting for the upright to praise him.
PSALM 33:1 NIV

Through him then let us continually offer up
a sacrifice of praise to God, that is, the fruit
of lips that acknowledge his name.
HEBREWS 13:15 ESV

"I called to the LORD, who is worthy of praise,
and have been saved from my enemies."
2 SAMUEL 22:4 NIV

Praise the LORD! Oh give thanks to the LORD, for
He is good; for His lovingkindness is everlasting.
PSALM 106:1 NASB

O LORD, you are my God; I will exalt you; I will
praise your name, for you have done wonderful
things, plans formed of old, faithful and sure.
ISAIAH 25:1 ESV

I will praise the name of God with a song;
I will magnify him with thanksgiving.
PSALM 69:30 ESV

I will praise the LORD, who counsels me;
even at night my heart instructs me.
PSALM 16:7 NIV

Oh give thanks to the LORD, for he is good;
for his steadfast love endures forever!
PSALM 118:29 ESV

For what you have done I will always praise you in
the presence of your faithful people. And I
will hope in your name, for your name is good.
PSALM 52:9 NIV

In God, whose word I praise, in God I
have put my trust; I shall not be afraid.
What can mere man do to me?
PSALM 56:4 NASB

Praise be to his glorious name forever;
may the whole earth be filled with
his glory. Amen and Amen.
PSALM 72:19 NIV

Praise to God, your praises bring;
Hearts, bow down, and voices sing!
Praises to the glorious One,
All His year of wonder done.

For His year of wonder done,
Praise to the all glorious One!
Hearts, bow down and voices, sing,
Praise and love to nature's king!
"PRAISE TO GOD, YOUR PRAISES BRING," WILLIAM C. GANNETT

Prayer

It boggles my mind when I think that the Creator of the universe would take the time to listen to my needs and speak to my heart. What a blessed privilege! I can come to You on good days and bad—to speak my mind, voice my concerns, lift words of praise, and simply spend time with You. Best of all, You want me to share my heart. You're not telling me to shush or to come back later. You actually long for me to pour out the things that are on my mind. I'm so grateful for my time with You, Father. Amen.

Do not be anxious about anything, but in
everything by prayer and supplication
with thanksgiving let your requests
be made known to God.

PHILIPPIANS 4:6 ESV

"But when you pray, go into your room
and shut the door and pray to your Father
who is in secret. And your Father who
sees in secret will reward you."

MATTHEW 6:6 ESV

"Call to me and I will answer you,
and will tell you great and hidden
things that you have not known."
JEREMIAH 33:3 ESV

So confess your sins to one another. Pray for
one another so that you might be healed.
The prayer of a godly person is powerful.
Things happen because of it.
JAMES 5:16 NIRV

"If you remain in me and my words
remain in you, ask whatever you wish,
and it will be done for you."
JOHN 15:7 NIV

You desire but do not have, so you kill.
You covet but you cannot get what you want,
so you quarrel and fight. You do not have
because you do not ask God.
JAMES 4:2 NIV

"And whatever things you ask in
prayer, believing, you will receive."
MATTHEW 21:22 NKJV

Pray, pray, when things go wrong,
And gloomy fears around you throng;
The loving God your voice will hear,
Look up to Him, He's always near.

Pray, pray though your eyes grow dim,
Go with your troubles straight to Him;
Pray, pray, for God understands;
Have faith, leaving all in His dear hands.

Pray, pray till faith grows strong,
And in your heart rings Heaven's song;
Till self shall die in pure desire,
And every thought to Him aspire.
"PRAY, PRAY," LIZZIE DEARMOND

Promises

You're an amazing Promise-Keeper, Lord! If You said it, it will happen. Many times, people have failed me. They've said one thing and done another, but You never have. That's how I know I can put my trust in You. Today I place every need—financial, emotional, physical, and relational, at Your feet. You will respond as only You can, in Your time and in Your way. Because I can trust Your promises, I choose to wait with expectation for what is to come. Praise You! Amen.

His divine power has granted to us all things
that pertain to life and godliness, through the
knowledge of him who called us to his own glory
and excellence, by which he has granted to us his
precious and very great promises, so that through
them you may become partakers of the divine
nature, having escaped from the corruption that
is in the world because of sinful desire.

2 Peter 1:3–4 esv

Then they believed his promises
and sang his praise.

Psalm 106:12 niv

For all the promises of God find their Yes
in him. That is why it is through him that
we utter our Amen to God for his glory.
2 CORINTHIANS 1:20 ESV

Not one word of all the good promises
that the LORD had made to the house
of Israel had failed; all came to pass.
JOSHUA 21:45 ESV

"And I will give you a new heart, and a
new spirit I will put within you. And I
will remove the heart of stone from your
flesh and give you a heart of flesh."
EZEKIEL 36:26 ESV

The Lord is not slow to fulfill his promise
as some count slowness, but is patient toward
you, not wishing that any should perish,
but that all should reach repentance.
2 PETER 3:9 ESV

"Lord, people find the will to live because you keep your promises. And my spirit also finds life in your promises. You brought me back to health. You let me live."

Isaiah 38:16 NIRV

Standing on the promises of Christ my king,
Through eternal ages let His praises ring;
Glory in the highest, I will shout and sing,
Standing on the promises of God.

Standing, standing,
Standing on the promises of God my Savior;
Standing, standing,
I'm standing on the promises of God.
"Standing on the Promises," R. Kelso Carter

Provision

Father, if You care for the birds above and the creatures below, if You provide for their daily needs, then who am I to get anxious about such things? You've already made provision, even before I ask. Shelter? You've got me covered. Food? You're cooking up a feast. Friends? You're drawing hearts, even now. There's not a single empty space in my life that You won't fill, if I just step back and stop trying to fill it myself. You are my Provider! I praise You for loving me so much. Amen.

And God is able to make all grace abound to you,
so that having all sufficiency in all things at all
times, you may abound in every good work.
2 Corinthians 9:8 esv

I have been young, and now am old, yet I have
not seen the righteous forsaken or his children
begging for bread. He is ever lending generously,
and his children become a blessing.
Psalm 37:25–26 esv

The LORD knows the days of the blameless,
and their heritage will remain forever; they
are not put to shame in evil times; in the
days of famine they have abundance.
PSALM 37:18–19 ESV

"Therefore I tell you, do not be anxious about
your life, what you will eat or what you will drink,
nor about your body, what you will put on. Is not
life more than food, and the body more than
clothing? Look at the birds of the air: they neither
sow nor reap nor gather into barns, and yet your
heavenly Father feeds them. Are you not of more
value than they? And which of you by being anxious
can add a single hour to his span of life? And why
are you anxious about clothing? Consider the lilies
of the field, how they grow: they neither toil
nor spin, yet I tell you, even Solomon in all his
glory was not arrayed like one of these."
MATTHEW 6:25–29 ESV

And my God will meet all your needs according
to the riches of his glory in Christ Jesus.
PHILIPPIANS 4:19 NIV

My hope is built on nothing less
Than Jesus' blood and righteousness.
I dare not trust the sweetest frame,
But wholly trust in Jesus' name.

On Christ the solid rock I stand,
All other ground is sinking sand;
All other ground is sinking sand.
"THE SOLID ROCK," EDWARD MOTE

Repentance

*Oh, how You long for Your children to walk in fullness,
Lord, but many times sin gets in the way. It creeps in, and
before I know it, I'm off course. What a gracious Father
You are! You tap me so gently on the shoulder and whisper,
"Turn around! You're going the wrong way." Your love,
grace, and mercy woo me and draw me back to You. What
a patient and loving Father You are, arms extended to
welcome me home, no matter what I've done. I'm so
grateful, Lord! Amen.*

"Repent therefore, and turn back,
that your sins may be blotted out."
ACTS 3:19 ESV

"I indeed baptize you with water unto
repentance, but He who is coming after
me is mightier than I, whose sandals I am
not worthy to carry. He will baptize you
with the Holy Spirit and fire."
MATTHEW 3:11 NKJV

Peter replied, "Repent and be baptized,
every one of you, in the name of Jesus Christ
for the forgiveness of your sins. And you
will receive the gift of the Holy Spirit."

ACTS 2:38 NIV

"I have not come to call the righteous,
but sinners, to repentance."

LUKE 5:32 NKJV

From that time Jesus began to preach, saying,
"Repent, for the kingdom of heaven is at hand."

MATTHEW 4:17 ESV

"I say to you that likewise there will be
more joy in heaven over one sinner
who repents than over ninety-nine just
persons who need no repentance."

LUKE 15:7 NKJV

"In the same way, I tell you, there is
rejoicing in the presence of the angels
of God over one sinner who repents."

LUKE 15:10 NIV

"I tell you, no; but unless you repent
you will all likewise perish."
LUKE 13:5 NKJV

"Even if they sin against you seven times
in a day and seven times come back to you
saying 'I repent,' you must forgive them."
LUKE 17:4 NIV

Repent, oh, repent, is the message
That rings from the Gospel today;
The voice is the voice of the Savior,
The Life and the Truth and the Way.

Repent, oh, repent and believe Him,
Who offers full pardon today;
'Tis Jesus who bids you receive Him,
There's no other way but this way.

Repentance will turn from wrongdoing,
To seek out the pathway of right,
And, trusting the mercy of Jesus,
Will walk in His glorious light.
"THERE'S NO OTHER WAY," JULIA H. JOHNSTON

Rest in Him

I'm so glad I can rest in You, Lord. This life is so crazy, so chaotic, that I often forget to slip away into Your presence for moments of refreshing. Oh, but You keep wooing me back! You long for me to find true rest, not just the kind that reinvigorates the body, but the kind that transforms my heart and mind. Today, I come willingly. I leave my cares behind and choose to rest in You, Lord. What a blissful opportunity! Amen.

Then, because so many people were coming and going that they did not even have a chance to eat, he said to them, "Come with me by yourselves to a quiet place and get some rest."
MARK 6:31 NIV

"Come to me, all who labor and are heavy laden, and I will give you rest. Take my yoke upon you, and learn from me, for I am gentle and lowly in heart, and you will find rest for your souls. For my yoke is easy, and my burden is light."
MATTHEW 11:28–30 ESV

Therefore, since the promise of entering his
rest still stands, let us be careful that none
of you be found to have fallen short of it.
HEBREWS 4:1 NIV

And he said, "My presence will go
with you, and I will give you rest."
EXODUS 33:14 ESV

And he said to them, "The Sabbath was
made for man, not man for the Sabbath."
MARK 2:27 ESV

By the seventh day God had finished the work he
had been doing; so on the seventh day he rested
from all his work. Then God blessed the seventh
day and made it holy, because on it he rested
from all the work of creating that he had done.
GENESIS 2:2–3 NIV

Let us therefore strive to enter that rest, so that no
one may fall by the same sort of disobedience.
HEBREWS 4:11 ESV

The L{ORD} is my shepherd, I shall not want.
He makes me lie down in green pastures;
He leads me beside quiet waters.
P{SALM} 23:1–2 N{ASB}

Come with all thy sorrow,
Weary wandering soul!
Come to Him who loves thee—
He will make thee whole.

There is rest in Jesus,
Sweet, sweet rest;
There is rest in Jesus,
Sweet, sweet rest.

He, thy strength in weakness,
Will thy refuge be;
Cast on Him thy burden—
He will care for thee.
"R{EST IN} J{ESUS}," F{ANNY} C{ROSBY}

Safety

You keep me safe, Lord! I don't have to fear terror by night when You're in charge (and You're always in charge). I can rest easy, knowing You're the best security guard ever. Today, I would ask that You bring peace to my heart during those moments when I start to feel afraid. Quench every fear. Remind me that I'm safe as long as I stick close to You. And teach me how to wear the armor You've given, that I might do my part as well. What an amazing Protector You are, Father! Amen.

The Lord will rescue me from every evil deed
and bring me safely into his heavenly kingdom.
To him be the glory forever and ever. Amen.
2 TIMOTHY 4:18 ESV

"Have I not commanded you? Be strong
and courageous. Do not be afraid; do not
be discouraged, for the LORD your God
will be with you wherever you go."
JOSHUA 1:9 NIV

In peace I will both lie down and sleep;
for you alone, O LORD, make me dwell in safety.

PSALM 4:8 ESV

The LORD is my strength and my shield;
my heart trusts in Him, and I am helped;
therefore my heart exults, and with my
song I shall thank Him.

PSALM 28:7 NASB

He who dwells in the shelter of the Most High
will abide in the shadow of the Almighty. I will say
to the LORD, "My refuge and my fortress, my God,
in whom I trust." For he will deliver you from the
snare of the fowler and from the deadly pestilence.
He will cover you with his pinions, and under
his wings you will find refuge; his faithfulness is
a shield and buckler. You will not fear the terror
of the night, nor the arrow that flies by day, nor
the pestilence that stalks in darkness, nor the
destruction that wastes at noonday. A thousand
may fall at your side, ten thousand at your right
hand, but it will not come near you.

PSALM 91:1–7 ESV

Put on the whole armor of God, that you may be able to stand against the schemes of the devil.

EPHESIANS 6:11 ESV

Safe in the arms of Jesus,
Safe on His gentle breast,
There by His love o'ershaded,
Sweetly my soul shall rest.
Hark! 'tis the voice of angels,
Borne in a song to me.
Over the fields of glory,
Over the jasper sea.

Safe in the arms of Jesus,
Safe on His gentle breast
There by His love o'ershaded,
Sweetly my soul shall rest.
"SAFE IN THE ARMS OF JESUS," FANNY CROSBY

Self-Control

Father, I'm always blaming my lack of self-control for things I should be doing. I say I can't watch what I eat, but I can. I say I can't keep my mouth from spouting off nonsense and gossip, but I can. There are so many areas of my life that need to be brought under control, Lord. So, today I will give it my best shot. I'll submit to the process. I'll need Your help, Father! Self-control alone won't cut it, I know. But with Your hand in mind, I'll turn these situations around. Praise You for Your patience with me, Lord. Amen.

A man without self-control is like a
city broken into and left without walls.
PROVERBS 25:28 ESV

No temptation has overtaken you that is not
common to man. God is faithful, and he will not
let you be tempted beyond your ability, but with
the temptation he will also provide the way of
escape, that you may be able to endure it.
1 CORINTHIANS 10:13 ESV

For this very reason, make every effort to
supplement your faith with virtue, and virtue
with knowledge, and knowledge with self-control,
and self-control with steadfastness, and steadfastness
with godliness, and godliness with brotherly
affection, and brotherly affection with love.

2 Peter 1:5–7 esv

Do you not know that those who run in a race
all run, but only one receives the prize? Run in
such a way that you may win. Everyone who
competes in the games exercises self-control in
all things. They then do it to receive a perishable
wreath, but we an imperishable. Therefore I run in
such a way, as not without aim; I box in such a way,
as not beating the air; but I discipline my body and
make it my slave, so that, after I have preached to
others, I myself will not be disqualified.

1 Corinthians 9:24–27 nasb

The end of all things is at hand; therefore
be self-controlled and sober-minded
for the sake of your prayers.

1 Peter 4:7 esv

Be sober-minded; be watchful. Your adversary
the devil prowls around like a roaring lion,
seeking someone to devour.
1 PETER 5:8 ESV

Cause me to walk in Christ my Way;
And I Thy statutes shall fulfill,
In every point Thy law obey,
And perfectly perform Thy will.

Within me Thy good Spirit place,
Spirit of health, and love, and power;
Plant in me Thy victorious grace,
And sin shall never enter more.
"GIVE ME A NEW, A PERFECT HEART," CHARLES WESLEY

Shame

Father, You bring correction in such a gentle way. You don't shame me or beat me over the head until I get things right. What a loving Father You are, so merciful and kind. When I go through seasons of shame, may I always run straight into Your arms, express my sorrows, and then be washed clean once again. My shame-filled days are over, Lord, thanks to You. May I walk in purity and reverence, head held high. Amen.

Instead of your shame you will receive a
double portion, and instead of disgrace you
will rejoice in your inheritance. And so you
will inherit a double portion in your land,
and everlasting joy will be yours.
ISAIAH 61:7 NIV

But the LORD GOD helps me; therefore I have not
been disgraced; therefore I have set my face like a
flint, and I know that I shall not be put to shame.
ISAIAH 50:7 ESV

If we confess our sins, He is faithful and
righteous to forgive us our sins and to
cleanse us from all unrighteousness.
1 JOHN 1:9 NASB

I sought the LORD, and he answered me
and delivered me from all my fears. Those
who look to him are radiant, and their
faces shall never be ashamed.
PSALM 34:4–5 ESV

I trust in you; do not let me be put to shame,
nor let my enemies triumph over me.
PSALM 25:2 NIV

No one who trusts in you will ever be
disgraced, but disgrace comes to those
who try to deceive others.
PSALM 25:3 NLT

In you, LORD, I have taken refuge; let me never be put to shame; deliver me in your righteousness.

PSALM 31:1 NIV

For this reason I also suffer these things, but I am not ashamed; for I know whom I have believed and I am convinced that He is able to guard what I have entrusted to Him until that day.

2 TIMOTHY 1:12 NASB

For in Scripture it says: "See, I lay a stone in Zion, a chosen and precious cornerstone, and the one who trusts in him will never be put to shame."

1 PETER 2:6 NIV

Defend me, Lord, from shame,
For still I trust in Thee;
Since just and righteous is Thy name,
From trouble set me free.
O Lord, in mercy hear,
Deliver me with speed;
Be my defense and refuge near,
My help in time of need.

"DEFEND ME, LORD, FROM SHAME," THE PSALTER

Sleep

Ah, blessed sleep! Some of my favorite moments of the day are found in drifting off to that sacred place, deep in slumber and free from the anxieties and cares of life. I'm so glad You designed the human body to need sleep, Lord. Those hours of rest are blissful. How close to You I feel as my eyelids grow heavy, Father. You watch over me, even while I slumber. Praise You, Lord! Amen.

If you lie down, you will not be afraid;
when you lie down, your sleep will be sweet.
PROVERBS 3:24 ESV

So the LORD God caused him to fall into a deep
sleep. While the man was sleeping, the LORD
God took out one of the man's ribs. Then the
LORD God closed the opening in the man's side.
GENESIS 2:21 NIRV

Sweet is the sleep of a laborer, whether
he eats little or much, but the full stomach
of the rich will not let him sleep.
ECCLESIASTES 5:12 ESV

I lie down and sleep. I wake up again,
because the Lord takes care of me.
Psalm 3:5 nirv

I go to bed and sleep in peace,
because, Lord, only you keep me safe.
Psalm 4:8 ncv

You keep him in perfect peace whose mind
is stayed on you, because he trusts in you.
Trust in the Lord forever.
Isaiah 26:3–4 esv

After hearing that, I, Jeremiah, woke up and looked
around. My sleep had been very pleasant.
Jeremiah 31:26 ncv

Sleep, my love, and peace attend thee,
All through the night;
Guardian angels God will lend thee,
All through the night;
Soft the drowsy hours are creeping,
Hill and dale in slumber sleeping;
Love alone his watch is keeping—
All through the night.
"All Through the Night," Harold E. Boulton

Spiritual Growth

Father, I don't want to grow stagnant. I want to move forward with You. I'm on such a learning curve, Lord, but You're a gentle Teacher, always encouraging me to grow in my faith. Help me, I pray. Lead me to the right Bible studies, the best mentors, and the perfect church. May I blossom and develop as a child of the King! Amen.

But grow in the grace and knowledge of our Lord
and Savior Jesus Christ. To him be the glory
both now and to the day of eternity. Amen.
2 Peter 3:18 esv

For this reason, since the day we heard about
you, we have not stopped praying for you.
We continually ask God to fill you with the
knowledge of his will through all the wisdom
and understanding that the Spirit gives, so that
you may live a life worthy of the Lord and
please him in every way: bearing fruit in every
good work, growing in the knowledge of God.
Colossians 1:9–10 niv

And I am sure of this, that he who began
a good work in you will bring it to
completion at the day of Jesus Christ.
PHILIPPIANS 1:6 ESV

Blessed is the man who walks not in the
counsel of the wicked, nor stands in the way
of sinners, nor sits in the seat of scoffers; but
his delight is in the law of the LORD, and on his
law he meditates day and night. He is like a tree
planted by streams of water that yields its fruit
in its season, and its leaf does not wither.
In all that he does, he prospers.
PSALM 1:1–3 ESV

All Scripture is God-breathed and is useful for
teaching, rebuking, correcting and training in
righteousness, so that the servant of God may
be thoroughly equipped for every good work.
2 TIMOTHY 3:16–17 NIV

Therefore let us leave the elementary doctrine of Christ and go on to maturity, not laying again a foundation of repentance from dead works and of faith toward God, and of instruction about washings, the laying on of hands, the resurrection of the dead, and eternal judgment.

HEBREWS 6:1–2 ESV

And may the Lord cause you to increase and abound in love for one another, and for all people, just as we also do for you; so that He may establish your hearts without blame in holiness before our God and Father at the coming of our Lord Jesus with all His saints.

1 THESSALONIANS 3:12–13 NASB

Grow like Jesus, He is love,
He is pure and holy;
You may be like Christ above,
Though your life be lowly.

Grow like Jesus, He is kind,
Patient, sweet, and tender;
None who seek Him fail to find,
He is our defender.

"GROW LIKE JESUS," JULIA H. JOHNSTON

Strength

I'm so glad I don't have to rely on my own strength, Lord. I can fake it for a while, but we both know that I eventually crater and give way to anxiety. You're the Strong One, Father! With just a word, You move mountains, open doors, and guard my every step. And You breathe that strength into me so that I can stand strong instead of crumbling. I'm so grateful for a God who works overtime to grow me into a believer who's strengthened from the inside out. Praise You for that! Amen.

I can do all things through
him who strengthens me.
PHILIPPIANS 4:13 ESV

Fear not, for I am with you; be not dismayed,
for I am your God; I will strengthen you,
I will help you, I will uphold you with
my righteous right hand.
ISAIAH 41:10 ESV

It is God who arms me with strength
and keeps my way secure.
PSALM 18:32 NIV

LORD, you gave me strength to fight the battle.
You made my enemies humble in front of me.
PSALM 18:39 NIRV

The LORD is my strength and my shield; my heart
trusts in Him, and I am helped; therefore my heart
exults, and with my song I shall thank Him.
PSALM 28:7 NASB

God is our refuge and strength,
always ready to help in times of trouble.
PSALM 46:1 NLT

Be strong, and let your heart take
courage, all you who wait for the LORD!
PSALM 31:24 ESV

In a loud voice they were saying: "Worthy is the Lamb, who was slain, to receive power and wealth and wisdom and strength and honor and glory and praise!"

REVELATION 5:12 NIV

Rise in the strength of God,
And face life's uphill way,
The steps which other feet have trod
You tread today.

Press onward, upward still,
To win your way at last,
With better hope and stronger will
Than in the past.

"RISE IN THE STRENGTH OF GOD," ADA R. GREENAWAY

Thankfulness

*Father, I often forget to thank You for the daily blessings
You provide. I overlook them, Lord. Please forgive me!
You're worthy of my praise and thanksgiving, Father,
not just for what You do, but for who You are. You're the
Creator of all, a loving Father, and the best Friend I'll ever
have. You provide for my every need and bring comfort
when I'm down. You're truly my All in All, and I'm so
grateful, Lord. Amen.*

Give thanks in all circumstances; for this
is the will of God in Christ Jesus for you.
1 Thessalonians 5:18 esv

Oh give thanks to the Lord, for he is good,
for his steadfast love endures forever!
Psalm 107:1 esv

Devote yourselves to prayer, keeping alert
in it with an attitude of thanksgiving.
Colossians 4:2 nasb

Let us come into his presence with
thanksgiving; let us make a joyful
noise to him with songs of praise!
PSALM 95:2 ESV

I will offer to you the sacrifice of thanksgiving
and call on the name of the LORD.
PSALM 116:17 ESV

We are receiving a kingdom that can't be shaken.
So let us be thankful. Then we can worship
God in a way that pleases him. Let us worship
him with deep respect and wonder.
HEBREWS 12:28 NIRV

The one who observes the day, observes it in
honor of the Lord. The one who eats, eats in
honor of the Lord, since he gives thanks to
God, while the one who abstains, abstains in
honor of the Lord and gives thanks to God.
ROMANS 14:6 ESV

Sing to the LORD with grateful praise;
make music to our God on the harp.
PSALM 147:7 NIV

"But I will sacrifice to You with the voice of
thanksgiving. That which I have vowed
I will pay. Salvation is from the LORD."
JONAH 2:9 NASB

Thanks to God for my Redeemer,
Thanks for all Thou dost provide!
Thanks for times now but a memory,
Thanks for Jesus by my side!
Thanks for pleasant, balmy springtime,
Thanks for dark and stormy fall!
Thanks for tears by now forgotten,
Thanks for peace within my soul!

Thanks for prayers that Thou hast answered,
Thanks for what Thou dost deny!
Thanks for storms that I have weathered,
Thanks for all Thou dost supply!
Thanks for pain, and thanks for pleasure,
Thanks for comfort in despair!
Thanks for grace that none can measure,
Thanks for love beyond compare!
"THANKS TO GOD," AUGUST L. STORM

Thoughts

*Oh, how my thoughts can wander, Lord! Instead of
focusing on You, they drift to my problems, my woes.
Help me rein in my thoughts today, Lord. I don't want
to hyper-focus on the negative. I don't want to give in to
anxieties. Transform my thinking, I pray. Give me Your
thoughts. Help me to see things the way You see them. May
every thought be rooted and grounded in You, Lord. Amen.*

Do not be conformed to this world, but be
transformed by the renewal of your mind, that by
testing you may discern what is the will of God,
what is good and acceptable and perfect.
ROMANS 12:2 ESV

Finally, brothers, whatever is true, whatever is
honorable, whatever is just, whatever is pure,
whatever is lovely, whatever is commendable,
if there is any excellence, if there is anything
worthy of praise, think about these things.
PHILIPPIANS 4:8 ESV

Therefore, holy brothers and sisters,
who share in the heavenly calling,
fix your thoughts on Jesus, whom we
acknowledge as our apostle and high priest.
Hebrews 3:1 niv

For the word of God is alive and active. Sharper
than any double-edged sword, it penetrates even
to dividing soul and spirit, joints and marrow;
it judges the thoughts and attitudes of the heart.
Hebrews 4:12 niv

Think about things that are in heaven.
Don't think about things that are only on earth.
Colossians 3:2 nirv

You keep him in perfect peace whose mind
is stayed on you, because he trusts in you.
Isaiah 26:3 esv

In your relationships with one another,
have the same mindset as Christ Jesus.
PHILIPPIANS 2:5 NIV

Then you will experience God's peace,
which exceeds anything we can understand.
His peace will guard your hearts and minds
as you live in Christ Jesus.
PHILIPPIANS 4:7 NLT

Therefore, with minds that are alert and fully sober,
set your hope on the grace to be brought to you
when Jesus Christ is revealed at his coming.
1 PETER 1:13 NIV

You were taught to be made
new in your thinking.
EPHESIANS 4:23 NIRV

O could our thoughts and wishes fly
Above these gloomy shades,
To those bright worlds beyond the sky,
Which sorrow ne'er invades!

Lord, send a beam of light divine,
To guide our upward aim!
With one reviving touch of thine,
Our languid hearts inflame.
"O COULD OUR THOUGHTS AND WISHES FLY," ANNE STEELE

Trust

How many times I've put my trust in my own abilities, only to be disappointed, Lord. Today, I choose to shift my focus. I'll place my trust in You. You've never let me down in the past and I know You won't now either. Thank You for being a trustworthy Father, someone I can truly count on, no matter what I'm going through. Amen.

When I am afraid, I put my trust in you. In God, whose word I praise, in God I trust; I shall not be afraid. What can flesh do to me?

PSALM 56:3–4 ESV

Those who know your name trust in you, for you, LORD, have never forsaken those who seek you.

PSALM 9:10 NIV

I will say of the LORD, "He is my refuge and my fortress, my God, in whom I trust."

PSALM 91:2 NIV

But I trust in your unfailing love;
my heart rejoices in your salvation.
PSALM 13:5 NIV

You keep him in perfect peace whose mind
is stayed on you, because he trusts in you.
Trust in the LORD forever, for the LORD
GOD is an everlasting rock.
ISAIAH 26:3–4 ESV

Yet You are He who brought me forth
from the womb; You made me trust
when upon my mother's breasts.
PSALM 22:9 NASB

Commit your way to the LORD;
trust in him, and he will act.
PSALM 37:5 ESV

In God I trust and am not afraid.
What can man do to me?
PSALM 56:11 NIV

He put a new song in my mouth, a song
of praise to our God; many will see and
fear and will trust in the LORD.
PSALM 40:3 NASB

May the God of hope fill you with all joy and peace
as you trust in him, so that you may overflow
with hope by the power of the Holy Spirit.
ROMANS 15:13 NIV

'Tis so sweet to trust in Jesus,
And to take Him at His word;
Just to rest upon His promise,
And to know, "Thus says the Lord!"

Jesus, Jesus, how I trust Him!
How I've proved Him o'er and o'er;
Jesus, Jesus, precious Jesus!
O for grace to trust Him more!

I'm so glad I learned to trust Thee,
Precious Jesus, Savior, friend;
And I know that Thou art with me,
Wilt be with me to the end.
"'TIS SO SWEET TO TRUST IN JESUS," LOUISA M. R. STEAD

Wisdom

*I'm learning, Lord! There's a difference between worldly
knowledge and godly wisdom. Knowledge is good, but
wisdom that streams down from Your heart is even better.
Draw me close so that I can learn from You, Father. I want
the wisdom that only You can bring. Amen.*

If any of you lacks wisdom, let him ask God,
who gives generously to all without reproach,
and it will be given him.
JAMES 1:5 ESV

"To God belong wisdom and power;
counsel and understanding are his."
JOB 12:13 NIV

The way of a fool is right in his own eyes,
but a wise man listens to advice.
PROVERBS 12:15 ESV

My mouth will speak words of wisdom; the
meditation of my heart will give you understanding.
PSALM 49:3 NIV

Don't bother to talk about coral and jasper.
Wisdom is worth far more than rubies.
JOB 28:18 NIRV

Intelligent people are always ready to learn.
Their ears are open for knowledge.
PROVERBS 18:15 NLT

Behold, You desire truth in the innermost
being, and in the hidden part You will
make me know wisdom.
PSALM 51:6 NASB

The fear of the LORD is the beginning of
wisdom; all who follow his precepts have good
understanding. To him belongs eternal praise.
PSALM 111:10 NIV

Whoever restrains his words has knowledge, and
he who has a cool spirit is a man of understanding.
Even a fool who keeps silent is considered wise;
when he closes his lips, he is deemed intelligent.
PROVERBS 17:27–28 ESV

Wisdom shouts in the street,
she lifts her voice in the square.
PROVERBS 1:20 NASB

Do not forsake wisdom, and she will protect you;
love her, and she will watch over you.
PROVERBS 4:6 NIV

"I am wisdom, and I have good judgment.
I also have knowledge and good sense."
PROVERBS 8:12 NCV

O boundless Wisdom, God most high,
O Maker of the earth and sky,
Who bid'st the parted waters flow
In heaven above, on earth below.

Let faith discern the eternal Light
Beyond the darkness of the night,
And through the mists of falsehood see
The path of truth revealed by Thee.

O Father, that we ask be done,
Through Jesus Christ, Thine only Son;
Who, with the Holy Ghost and Thee,
Doth live and reign eternally.
"O BOUNDLESS WISDOM, GOD MOST HIGH," AUTHOR UNKNOWN

Work

How we enjoy the fruit of our labors, Lord! Whether we're pouring ourselves into a project at work, caring for our children, or delving into a craft or redecorating project, we enjoy the process of "doing." The very act of busying ourselves in worthy work can calm life's anxieties. You've given us a desire to work, Father, and I'm grateful for it. May I do all I can to labor for Your causes, Lord. Amen.

Whatever you do, work at it with
all your heart, as working for the
Lord, not for human masters.
COLOSSIANS 3:23 NIV

From the fruit of their lips people are
filled with good things, and the work
of their hands brings them reward.
PROVERBS 12:14 NIV

You will enjoy the fruit of your labor.
How joyful and prosperous you will be!
PSALM 128:2 NLT

The appetite of laborers works for
them; their hunger drives them on.
PROVERBS 16:26 NIV

All hard work brings a profit,
but mere talk leads only to poverty.
PROVERBS 14:23 NIV

Then God blessed the seventh day and made
it holy, because on it he rested from all the
work of creating that he had done.
GENESIS 2:3 NIV

"But you, take courage! Do not let your hands
be weak, for your work shall be rewarded."
2 CHRONICLES 15:7 NRSV

Those who work their land will have abundant
food, but those who chase fantasies have no sense.
PROVERBS 12:11 NIV

He told them, "The harvest is plentiful, but the
workers are few. Ask the Lord of the harvest,
therefore, to send out workers into his harvest field."
LUKE 10:2 NIV

"We must work the works of Him who sent Me as long as it is day; night is coming when no one can work."

JOHN 9:4 NASB

"Stay there, eating and drinking whatever they give you, for the worker deserves his wages."

LUKE 10:7 NIV

Let us work and pray together,
With a firm and strong endeavor,
Hearts and hands united ever
In the service of the Lord;
In His constant love abiding,
And to Him our all confiding,
With His gentle hand still guiding
We shall conquer through His word.

In the dawn of life's fair morning,
With its smile our path adorning,
Let us heed the Master's warning:
"Time is flying, work today."
See the royal host advancing,
Armed with zeal, and upward glancing,
Full of hope and joy entrancing;
Let us quickly haste away.

"WORK AND PRAY," FANNY CROSBY

Worry

I don't want to be a worrywart, Lord! I want to ease my thoughts and my heart by casting all of my cares on You. That's what I choose to do today. Those things that have been distracting me, weighing me down? I place them at Your feet. You're the great Burden-Bearer, Worry-Carrier. Your shoulders are strong enough to bear it all, Father, and I'm so grateful to be relieved of the weight. How I praise You! Amen.

Do not worry about anything, but pray and
ask God for everything you need, always giving
thanks. And God's peace, which is so great
we cannot understand it, will keep your
hearts and minds in Christ Jesus.
PHILIPPIANS 4:6–7 NCV

You keep him in perfect peace whose mind
is stayed on you, because he trusts in you.
ISAIAH 26:3 ESV

"Can any one of you by worrying
add a single hour to your life?"
MATTHEW 6:27 NIV

Cast your burden on the LORD,
and he will sustain you; he will never
permit the righteous to be moved.
PSALM 55:22 ESV

Set your minds on things that are above,
not on things that are on earth.
COLOSSIANS 3:2 ESV

I have set the LORD always before me; because
he is at my right hand, I shall not be shaken.
PSALM 16:8 ESV

Say to those who have an anxious heart,
"Be strong; fear not! Behold, your God will
come with vengeance, with the recompense
of God. He will come and save you."
ISAIAH 35:4 ESV

"Let not your hearts be troubled.
Believe in God; believe also in me."
John 14:1 esv

When the cares of my heart are many,
your consolations cheer my soul.
Psalm 94:19 esv

Day by day, and with each passing moment,
Strength I find, to meet my trials here;
Trusting in my Father's wise bestowment,
I've no cause for worry or for fear.
He whose heart is kind beyond all measure
Gives unto each day what He deems best—
Lovingly, its part of pain and pleasure,
Mingling toil with peace and rest.
"Day by Day," Karolina Sandell-Berg

Worship

Oh, how I worship You, Lord! With my whole heart, I honor You. You are worthy of the highest praise, not just on days when everything is going my way, but even when I'm down in the dumps or riddled with anxiety. There is none like You, Father! You're perfect in all Your ways, trustworthy and true. All of my praise, honor, and glory goes to You! Amen.

"God is spirit, and those who worship
him must worship in spirit and truth."
JOHN 4:24 ESV

All the ends of the earth will remember
and turn to the LORD, and all the families
of the nations will worship before You.
PSALM 22:27 NASB

"But the hour is coming, and is now here,
when the true worshipers will worship the
Father in spirit and truth, for the Father
is seeking such people to worship him."
JOHN 4:23 ESV

Oh come, let us worship and bow down;
let us kneel before the LORD, our Maker!
PSALM 95:6 ESV

Jesus answered, "It is written: 'Worship
the Lord your God and serve him only.'"
LUKE 4:8 NIV

All the nations you have made will
come and worship before you, Lord;
they will bring glory to your name.
PSALM 86:9 NIV

I appeal to you therefore, brothers, by the
mercies of God, to present your bodies as
a living sacrifice, holy and acceptable to
God, which is your spiritual worship.
ROMANS 12:1 ESV

Then the man said, "Lord, I believe,"
and he worshiped him.
JOHN 9:38 NIV

Worship the LORD in the splendor of his
holiness; tremble before him, all the earth.
PSALM 96:9 NIV

Ascribe to the LORD the glory due his name;
worship the LORD in the splendor of holiness.
PSALM 29:2 ESV

O worship the Lord in the beauty of holiness!
Bow down before Him, His glory proclaim;
With gold of obedience, and incense of lowliness,
Kneel and adore Him: the Lord is His name!

Low at His feet lay thy burden of carefulness,
High on His heart He will bear it for thee;
Comfort thy sorrows, and answer thy prayerfulness,
Guiding thy steps as may best for thee be.
"WORSHIP THE LORD IN THE BEAUTY
OF HOLINESS," JOHN S. B. MONSELL

More Bible Promise Book
Editions to Bless Your Heart. . .

The Bible Promise Book: 500 Scriptures to Bless a Woman's Heart

Barbour's Bible Promise Books are perennial bestsellers, with millions of copies in print. *The Bible Promise Book* is available in a lovely paperback edition featuring 500 scripture selections plus encouraging prayer starters to bless your heart. With 50 topics that matter most to you—including Comfort, Love, Faith, Worry, Worship, Courage, Joy, and Contentment—you can quickly and easily locate a topic that will speak to your needs.
Paperback / 978-1-68322-729-8 / $5.99

The Bible Promise Book: 500 Scriptures for a Heart-Shaped Life
(July 2019)

Here's a brand-new Bible Promise Book based on the daily devotional *The Heart-Shaped Life*. Featuring dozens of timely topics to help you live life "heart first"—including Attitude, Compassion, Generosity, Trust, Witness, and more—this book provides hundreds of scriptures to help you discover the path to the good life, which is love.
Paperback / 978-1-64352-042-1 / $5.99